These are the songs that have influenced my life more than any other. Behind every song is a story, and Ace Collins' meticulous research and wonderful writing have shown me just how my favorite inspirational and gospel songs came to be. Thanks, Ace, for the blessings!

Joe Bonsall, The Oak Ridge Boys

Everyone rejoices with a moving gospel song, and everyone enjoys a good story. Ace Collins masterfully blends the two to give readers an inspirational and insightful picture into the Christian musical genre that laid the foundation of rock, country, and blues.

John Hillman, Religion Correspondent
Arlington Morning News

If you've ever sung any of these old gospel favorites or just enjoyed listening to them, you'll thrill at the stories behind the songs: who wrote them, when, and why. It's all here and you're gonna love it.

Don Reid, The Statler Brothers

D1508787

Turn Your
Radio
On

DATE DUE

B 08			

Turn Your
Radio On

The stories behind gospel music's all-time greatest songs

Ace Collins

ZondervanPublishingHouse
Grand Rapids, Michigan

A Division of HarperCollinsPublishers

Turn Your Radio On
Copyright © 1999 by Ace Collins

Requests for information should be addressed to:

 ZondervanPublishingHouse
Grand Rapids, Michigan 49530

Library of Congress Cataloging-in-Publication Data

Collins, Ace.
    Turn your radio on: the stories behind Gospel music's all-time greatest songs /
Ace Collins.
      p. cm.
    ISBN 0-310-21153-0 (softcover)
    1. Hymns, English—United States—History and criticism.
  I. Title.
BV313.C65 1999
264'.23—dc21
                                                          99-24350
                                                            CIP

Interior design by Sherri L. Hoffman

Printed in the United States of America

99 00 01 02 03 04 05 06 /❖ DC/ 10 9 8 7 6 5 4 3 2 1

To the late

Marion Minser

and to every man and woman who has brought music
to small congregations on a volunteer basis.
Through their hours of dedication
they have not only brought beautiful music
to thousands of churches, but have also
led countless souls to Christ
through messages in song.

Contents

Introduction

G ospel songs are born of an intimate spiritual experience seemingly all but too personal to share. Yet while created to define an individual's special walk with God, a true gospel song can reach anyone. It literally paints the Christian story in strokes so bold that the message can be understood by the mind while being felt in the heart.

Gospel music is steeped in emotion, not logic. While gospel music may make people think, its real goal is to get them to feel. Gospel music doesn't just proclaim there is a God, it invites people to get to know the Lord as a friend.

Though often born out of tragedy, gospel songs seem always to bring joy. They leave those who have sung them and those who have heard them smiling. In almost any form gospel music is entertaining, but in its purest form a gospel song is a testimony leading the unsaved to Christ and believers to a closer walk with Jesus.

In this book are the stories behind sixty-five very special gospel songs. While the songs may have been made famous by the likes of Red Foley, the Blackwood Brothers, the Stamps Quartet, the Speer Family, Bessie Smith, George Beverly Shea, Ethel Waters, Elvis Presley, and a host of other well-known entertainers, they have also been sung just as wonderfully by millions of anonymous voices.

Some of these sixty-five gospel songs were written by legendary writers; others, by men and women who are all but completely unknown. Their musical productions vary from country songs, urban blues, African-American spirituals, and even rocking beats. Yet no matter who first sang these classics, who wrote them, or where they came from, they are each linked by a message centering on Christ and His amazing grace. Because of this theme, these songs are not just entertaining, they are soul-winning, life-changing tools.

It has been said that there is a song in every person. While this may or may not be true, it can be stated with some certainty that one or more of the songs in this book lives in the soul of every Christian. All over the world, the words, music, and messages of these songs are alive in hearts and guiding believers through both good and bad times. Best of all, they are there not only when you turn your radio on, but when you turn it off, too.

Amazing Grace

Although there are a host of different opinions about the roots of modern gospel music, there is no debate about the fact that true gospel music must possess a message that universally appeals to the masses and that each composition must present a uniquely individual testimony. Gospel is therefore a deeply personal music that seems always to originate in a single soul offering a message of hope that begs to transport a person to the highest reaches of heaven. And as long as there has been gospel music, there have been those souls who shared their most meaningful experiences through simple but sincere verse and song.

Long before the emergence of radio and recordings, even before America had emerged as a nation, John Newton's life was set on a course to spawn a musical style that would pave the way for religious music to be brought out of the hallowed halls of great cathedrals and sung in even the most modest of rural venues. For, like the gospel that Paul and the other apostles spread in the very first days of the Christian church, if the message was to reach the masses, it had to be heard in the real world by real sinners seeking a better life. And if there ever was a sinner who was living far from the church and its narrow way, it was the young sailor who would later pen the words to America's most beloved gospel song.

John Newton was a troubled, motherless boy who ran away from home before his teens and followed his father to the sea. Once on the waves the impressionable British-born lad quickly developed all the wild and vile ways of the sailors who became his friends and mentors. As a teen he was a fighter and a drinker and a respecter of little but the law of might. After a stint in the Royal Navy as a cabin boy, Newton spent much of the middle part of the eighteenth century as a seaman on a slave trader. Here he and his shipmates regularly acquired African men and women and transported them to a life of slavery in the New World. As could be quickly seen by the most casual observer, for John Newton, human life, even his own, meant little and was worth even less. By the time he was twenty most of those who knew John well wondered if there was even a tiny piece of a soul left to save in the young man's rugged body.

Like Paul, Newton was wholly transformed suddenly and violently. In 1748 he found himself on a ship being tossed and torn in a hurricane. As the twenty-three-year-old Newton helplessly watched the waves crash over the deck, he sensed that his life might quickly be coming to an end. Although he had watched scores of slaves die on long ocean voyages, and though he had even seen countless shipmates lost at sea, Newton had never faced his own mortality. Frightened beyond words, unable to control anything that was transpiring around him, and listening to the wailing and cursing of the doomed men around him, John remembered his late mother. As he thought of her, a memory of her faith took hold of him. Falling to his knees on the deck of the rolling ship, he turned to something he had seen his mother do on many occasions in her brief life. He prayed. Miraculously, even as he struggled to come up with words to purge the pain from his soul, the storm passed and the ship steadied itself. Yet even more startling to the crew than the sudden end to the violent storm was John Newton's urging them all to give thanks to God for this miracle.

Within a decade of his conversion Newton had fallen under the influence of the famed preacher Charles Wesley and had given his life to Christ in Christian service. While serving as a pastor in Olney, England, John set the story of his own deliverance from the storms of life in verse and shared the song of salvation with his congregation.

The first four stanzas of "Amazing Grace" have changed little since they were first published in 1779. Yet while the message was straight from the home of King James, the music we sing has a flavor that owes as much to the hills of Kentucky as it does to the meadows of Britain. When William Walker was preparing to publish his "Southern Harmony" songbook in 1835, he replaced the original musical score of Newton's verse with an American folk melody known as "Harmony Grove." It is this version, complete with an additional fifth stanza written by an unknown writer, that has become the most beloved of all "American" hymns (we do tend to claim it as our own) and the foundation for the growth and widespread acceptance of gospel music both here and around the world.

By the turn of the century "Amazing Grace" was sung in churches, camp meetings, revivals, and homes around the country. Because of its personal nature and universal but starkly individual message, this song even found acceptance outside the normal channels of religious music. The early black gospel singers W.M. Nix and Roberta Martin put real spiritual blues and soul into their performances of Newton's song as they took it to both religious and secular venues. Early southern gospel performers added a bit of twang and rousing four-part quartet harmonies and sang it in brush arbor meetings and at rural schoolhouses. The song survived the big band and rock-and-roll musical evolution, but, more than that, entertainers like Hank Williams and Elvis Presley, men who challenged the very fabric of accepted musical standards of their times, sang it in their live performances. And somehow, even in the midst of an explosion of new gospel music composers, songs, and publishers in the early sixties, this almost two-hundred-year-old standard remained one of the music's most personal and moving testimonies to the grace and power of God. Yet, even though the old hymn was deeply loved and its message revered by believers everywhere, few thought "Amazing Grace" would ever find its way onto a popular music chart. This seemed to be one stormy sea even John Newton's old standard couldn't ride.

In 1971, at the height of Vietnam War protests, racial discord, rioting in the streets, and widespread mistrust of the government, pop-folk performer Judy Collins recorded and released a single of John Newton's tribute to God's grace. At a time when acid rock and free love were influencing pop culture, at the very moment when millions wondered if the world wasn't willing itself into the fiery furnaces of hell, "Amazing Grace" rode the rock and pop charts longer than any other Judy Collins release. Thousands who had never set foot in a Sunday school classroom or heard a sermon were singing John Newton's universal message of God's grace.

A decade later "Amazing Grace" again found itself transported to new heights as it appeared in the last place most people would have expected to find it. When the fictional character of Mr. Spock died in the *Star Trek* movie *The Wrath of Khan*, the old standard was played at his funeral. Even in this science fiction projection of the future, it seems that God cared for the most alien of souls and that there was still a need for "amazing grace."

"Amazing Grace" has become more than a hymn, it has become a model challenging gospel songwriters to be personal and direct with their stories, as well as universal and timeless with their message. John Newton didn't just hit a chord when he penned his victorious words, he touched hearts and opened the door to acceptance of Christ and salvation not only for his generation but also for the many generations that have followed. And though they never met the author, surely all those who love gospel music today owe a great debt to a sailor who put his personal story of salvation into an amazing song.

Battle Hymn of the Republic

The tune to "Battle Hymn of the Republic" was introduced to Julia Ward Howe on a night in 1861 as she was riding in a horse-drawn coach through the nation's capital with her husband, Dr. Howe; a minister friend, Dr. James Freeman Clarke; and Governor Andrews of Massachusetts. The scene around them was chaotic. Thousands of Union troops were marching in every street preparing for a looming battle with thirteen slave states who had broken off and formed a new confederation. Abraham Lincoln was an unproved leader, and millions were questioning if the pending battles were worth the price the country would have to pay just to preserve a union.

As the party slowly made their way through the streets, Dr. Clarke noted a group of men gathered outside an inn singing "John Brown's body lies amouldering in the grave." Rather than inspire the minister's patriotic spirit, the image of a once proud man rotting in the soil disgusted him. He glanced toward the Howes and declared that a tune so robust should not be coupled with words so dismal.

The thoughts of death and destruction and the images of young men shooting each other on smoke-filled fields haunted Julia Howe. Although she tried to shake the scenes from her mind, she couldn't. Unable to sleep, she rose from her bed in a Washington hotel room, and with the tune from "John Brown's

Body" still echoing in her mind, she picked up pen and paper and jotted down a poem set to the cadence of that song:

> *Mine eyes have seen the glory of the coming of the Lord.*
> *He is trampling out the vineyards where the grapes of wrath*
>   *are stored,*
> *He has loosed the faithful lightning of his terrible swift*
>   *sword.*
> *His truth is marching on.*

At daybreak she showed the finished poem to her husband. Deeply moved, Dr. Howe encouraged her to polish it. She did so, and upon returning to her home in Boston, Julia shared "Mine Eyes Have Seen the Glory" with James T. Fields, the editor of *Atlantic Monthly*. He published it in an early 1862 issue of the magazine. Soon after that it was adopted by Union forces as their theme song.

In many ways it was ironic that "Battle Hymn of the Republic" would become a rallying point for the soldiers of the northern armies. The tune was actually born in South Carolina, and, until it had been coupled to "John Brown's Body," it was considered a southern folk melody.

Some fifty years after the Civil War ended, a daughter was born to a stevedore in New Orleans. She was singing in her church choir before she could read. By the time she was ten, her voice could bend the blues like that of the legendary Bessie Smith. Yet young Mahalia Jackson didn't really care much for the blues, they were too sad. She wanted to sing happy songs that made people feel good.

Migrating to Chicago in her teens, Mahalia worked as a maid until she coupled up with gospel songwriter and choir director Thomas A. Dorsey. Dorsey seemed convinced that Mahalia's voice came straight from heaven and therefore no one had the right to tamper with it. Not wanting to change her unique style and phrasing, Dorsey didn't even allow her to sing with his choir, take voice lessons, or work with other writers. He demanded that the young woman just "sing it the way she felt it."

During the Depression Jackson quickly rose to the ranks of the best-known female African-American gospel singers in the nation. Fronting for Dorsey's choirs, she cut records, appeared on radio, and brought the house down at the Apollo Theater. By 1950 she had toured Europe and sung for presidents and kings. To many, both white and black, she *was* gospel music. With her deliberate, carefully paced, dramatic renderings of songs such as "Move On Up a Little Higher" and "Keep Me Every Day," she led thousands to the Lord. Often imitated, she was never equaled.

Those who accompanied Jackson were awed not only by her voice but also by her presence. She never apologized for being a woman, being black, or being a Christian. She felt that these were all facets of what made her unique in God's eyes. She was such a strong woman of faith that even men who professed racist feelings bowed before her.

A child of the South, Mahalia Jackson took her place in the forefront of the battle for civil rights. A hundred years after Julia Ward Howe wrote the words to "Battle Hymn of the Republic," Mahalia sang the song in front of hundreds of thousands at civil-rights rallies, in churches, at banquets, at concerts, and in Billy Graham crusades. She transformed the old southern folk song and the inspired lyrics of a cultured Bostonian into one of the most powerful gospel offerings in history. For years considered just an anthem for choral groups, the "Battle Hymn of the Republic" became, because of Mahalia's treatment, one of the greatest gospel standards ever to be performed in musical circles.

The most wonderful thing about the way Mahalia sang "Battle Hymn" was that she never moved the piece at the same pace. As she performed, she prayed, allowing the Spirit to guide her emotions, her inflections, and her speed. Embracing each word to fully bring out its meaning, she brought new light to the song each time she sang it. One could hear her sing Howe's song a hundred times and never hear it the same way twice. For that reason, she held her audiences spellbound, thus allowing every audience to glory in the Lord.

It now seems appropriate that gospel music helped to identify a movement that led to the building of a bridge between all of God's people. It is just as appropriate that a southern-born black woman singer took the words that once rallied troops fighting for her ancestors' freedom and made them a testament of faith for all people of all races. Mahalia Jackson's gospel music was built on the faith of both white and black, and she blended it into a voice of universal belief in a color-blind God. While doing so, she also fully defined "Battle Hymn of the Republic."

Because He Lives

There may be a great deal of debate as to who is the greatest gospel music songwriter in history. Some will point to Thomas Dorsey, others to Ira Stanphill, Stuart Hamblen, or Albert Brumley. All of these men are certainly unique and deserve the praise given to them by gospel music's fans and critics. Yet when it comes to team writing, few will argue there has not been a better song writing partnership than that of Bill and Gloria Gaither. This married duo has not only turned out over three hundred inspirational classics, but through their work they have also bridged the gap between southern, black, and contemporary gospel music. Blessed with incredible talents and driven by missionary zeal, this couple has produced work that has resulted in countless souls accepting Christ as their personal Savior.

Bill had loved gospel music since his childhood. He grew up in Indiana, attending scores of southern gospel concerts and meeting countless quartet singers. As a teen he pitched his songs to groups such as the Weatherfords, the Speer Family, and the Blackwood Brothers. The first southern gospel quartet to fully latch onto Bill's new kind of gospel sound was the Imperials. In their role as backup singers for rock-and-roll legend Elvis Presley, the group introduced these entertainment people to Bill's music. This introduction would lead not only to Elvis's winning a Grammy with Bill's material but also to Gaither's quick rise from struggling songwriter to top writer in Christian music.

Gloria had met her future husband while attending Anderson College. After their wedding she joined Bill in teaching high school for several years. While they worked on perfecting their craft as songwriters, they performed both old standard songs and newly penned Christian songs in area churches. As their writing career became established, the couple quit teaching and devoted themselves full time to their music.

By the late sixties Bill and Gloria were distressed and disillusioned. The Vietnam War, the country's struggle with civil rights, the hippie movement, the free-sex and drug cultures, and violence on the streets and on television and movies had led them to feel trapped in a hopeless world of hate. They began to question what kind of lives their two young daughters could expect when they were adults. Was it even wise to bring a child into a world like this? To add to their feelings of despair, old friends had recently deserted them, and both Bill and Gloria were experiencing health problems. Then, to top it all off, Gloria became pregnant with their third child. The couple's fears and doubts deepened.

The winter of 1969 would be the longest of their lives. The snows piled higher, the cold wind blew harder, and the skies stayed gray week after week. It was not the kind of scene that inspired much hope for their future.

In the spring of that year Bill and his father walked out to inspect a newly paved parking lot behind his office. The construction workers had spent weeks digging up the soil, packing it down, rolling out loads of gravel and then covering the area with several coats of asphalt. Bill was more than satisfied with the work and was returning inside when his father spotted something he couldn't believe and had to point out to his son. In the middle of the newly paved parking lot a tiny blade of grass had pushed aside layers of dirt, rock, and tar to reach the world that lay above. It had such a strong will to live that it had overcome all the odds to fulfill its destiny.

On July 19, 1970, Benjamin Gaither was born. Although Bill and Gloria knew the world would no doubt heap mounds of problems on this child throughout his life, they had been renewed in their Christian faith by the determination of a tiny blade of grass. The world was in chaos, but it had been so also in Christ's time and every century since. With faith, Benjamin would not just endure, but prosper.

After the couple brought their child home, they sat down to work out a tribute to the honor God had bestowed on them as parents. With a zeal in their hearts and the joy of life flooding their souls, they wrote the lyrics and score for a resounding song of tribute to the enduring love and power of Christ as realized by the birth of a child.

The Gaithers have never turned away from their faith. They have never asked how or when God's blessings would fill their lives and make them fruitful; rather, they have been consumed by doing what can be done now. When they are asked why they work so hard to bring the story of Jesus to so many, their thoughts often go back to a single blade of grass fighting to get into a hostile world and they answer, "Because He lives."

Beyond the Sunset

$\mathcal{V}$irgil P. Brock was one of gospel music's pioneer song-writers and singing-convention teachers. Composing hundreds of songs and leading schools of music even when he was in his nineties, Brock seemed to always have joy in his heart and a spring in his step. Friends described him as the most optimistic man they had ever met.

Yet in 1936, at the heart of the Great Depression, even Brock's optimism must have been tested. Life was tough for most who frequented the schools and churches where Virgil and his wife, Blanche, taught. Although the government had mobilized tens of thousands of people in work programs such as the W.P.A. and C.C.C., it just wasn't enough. In Oklahoma and Arkansas and other states scores of families who had already lost everything but their pride had been forced off their farms by bankers and mortgage holders. As former millionaires sold apples on New York street corners and ranchers became fruit pickers, is it any wonder that many were questioning if the American way of life was doomed?

Watching faith slowly drain out of those who had once seemed to be so hopeful must have deeply affected Brook. Everywhere he went, people looked tired, both spiritually and physically. All they had to hang onto were the lessons they had learned in Sunday school and the messages they had heard in church. And sometimes it seemed that these lessons weren't enough.

At about the time John Steinbeck began to write *The Grapes of Wrath*, Virgil and Blanche were invited to spend a few days at the Winona Lake, Indiana, home of gospel music publisher

Homer Rodeheaver. With the Brocks were Virgil's cousin Horace Burr, who had been blind since birth, and his wife.

There, in the midst of the woods, the couples were allowed to escape a world filled with bad news and submerge themselves in the luxury of life with no problems. This rest brought a peaceful calmness that had eluded the Brocks as they had desperately journeyed from one town to another teaching music.

After supper one evening, Virgil and his wife were caught up in a technicolor scene unfolding just outside their window. As the summer sun was setting, the multicolored hues of the sky reflected across the placid surface of the lake, and just above the sun, from a huge thundercloud they could see flashing lightning and hear claps of thunder. This amazing convergence of natural events so captured the couple's attention that they forgot that the Burrs were sitting with them.

For several minutes, as the sun sank lower in the sky, nothing was said. Finally, just as the sun's rays disappeared and were replaced by storm clouds, Horace Burr commented, "That was the most beautiful sunset I have ever seen."

After a moment of awkward silence he added, "Oh, I can see. It may be through others' words, but I can see the sunset. Better yet, I can see beyond it."

The thought of a blind man "seeing" inspired the Brocks to immediately try to write down the glory of what they had just witnessed. With the magnificent beauty of the sunset still fresh in their minds, Virgil and Blanche jotted down lines in an almost rapid-fire fashion. For a song whose lyrics number only 111 words, the story it tells is monumental. Each stanza embraces a different theme, but they all fit together in a manner that makes them "four-square" strong.

The first stanza deals with the pain and toil of working in an unforgiving world. On the surface the lines seem to have been written for the Brocks themselves, for their lives were hard and their days offered few rewards. For them the time after sunset represented a chance to rest. Yet underneath these lines are images of the hope that faith in Christ offers at times when we seem to be getting nowhere.

The second stanza builds on this theme but brings an additional message of life without grief, storms, or fear. This place, just beyond death, is an eternal world where sunshine will light everlasting days of glory.

The fear of the unknown, both in life and in death, is dealt with in the third stanza. The promise of having a Father's hand to guide each believer through every test and trial on earth, as well as through death and into glory, is a message that both young and old can grasp and cling to at any time.

Finally, the final stanza speaks of a reunion. Such a thought must have meant a great deal not only to those who had lost loved ones in death, but also to those who were now separated from loved ones by thousands of miles because of the consequences of the Great Depression. "Beyond the Sunset" gave each of them the hope that any separation was only temporary.

As if by magic, "Beyond the Sunset" seemed to go directly from the Brocks' pen to the hearts of the American people. Published by Rodeheaver, within months the song found its way into churches and homes across the nation. It is one of the few gospel songs that seems meant for congregational singing, yet its special message of faith is also uniquely personal.

The apostle Paul often wrote about the promises and gifts that Christ has offered us. Paul would have probably gloried in the words of Virgil and Blanche Brocks as much as anyone. For, like Horace Burr, the apostle had once been blind, but thanks to faith in the Lord Jesus he could see far beyond the sunset.

Can the Circle Be Unbroken?

*T*here is a centuries-old tie between American gospel and country music and traditional English folk songs. In the early days of our nation's history, the American upper class may have listened to the classical music of Europe, but the rural settlers were revising English folk music, adapting it to their own life stories. Many of the great gospel and country tunes were brought to America by men and women fleeing England's oppression and religious persecution. In a very real sense, this rural music, sung in both homes and churches, became an oral history of tragedy, suffering, hope, and faith. It was also a way of connecting with the home and loved ones they had left behind across the sea. It was music that helped to keep the tie of faith unbroken.

Country music legend A.P. Carter sought out many of these folk tunes and their new lyrics when he was looking for performance material for the Carter Family. Throughout the late twenties and early thirties the group had a string of country hits based on the melding of English folk music with the American experience. Yet even A.P.'s efforts to find new folk songs couldn't keep the group on top forever.

The Carter Family began to fall off the popular charts by 1935. Although it was not reported, one of the causes for the group's lackluster performances could be traced to the fact that A.P. and Sara had divorced. They still worked together, but their lives began to go in very different directions. Many believe it was the failure of his marriage that drew A.P. to an Ada Haberson and Charles Gabriel hymn, "Will the Circle Be Unbroken?" Like so many other songs that he came to love, this song could trace its musical roots to English folk songs.

A.P. took the heart of the chorus of "Will the Circle Be Unbroken?" and worked in his own ideas for new stanzas. When he was finished, he had changed the song's title and tag line to "Can the Circle Be Unbroken?"

The song was really the story of a very sad funeral. In each stanza those who had gathered to say good-bye to their loved one were questioning if they would ever be reunited. They wanted to know if there would be a time—by and by—when their family circle would once again be unbroken. If A.P. had intended this message to sway Sara to come back to him, the song failed. Yet while it might not have moved Sara, it did move millions of music fans.

"Can the Circle Be Unbroken?" was a huge seller in the rural South and Midwest. A big reason for its success may have been the suffering created by the Great Depression. As families were torn apart by poverty and despair, as men and women packed up their belongings and moved across the country looking for work, "Can the Circle Be Unbroken?" became a personal statement of faith. It should not be surprising that by the end of the decade the song had become one of the most popular funeral hymns. It spoke to those grieving families as few songs ever had.

Beyond its emotional content, the song brought to the forefront the gospel and its spiritual elements that had helped to shape early country music. By and large those who sang country music began singing in church. Gospel standards were the foundation that led to their seeking out other forms of musical expression. And from time to time, on stage shows and in recordings, it was to gospel music that almost all of them returned.

"Can the Circle Be Unbroken?" made it to #17 on the pop charts in 1935. It stayed on radio play lists for a while, then slowly drifted out of commercial music and into churches, revivals, and all-night singings. Yet because country music will never be able to fully separate itself from its gospel background, just about the time the song was being forgotten by those singing gospel music, it reappeared as a country music hit.

By 1968 former rock singer Carl Perkins was a part of the Johnny Cash Show. Cash had given Perkins a job and helped pull the singer out of an almost fatal addiction to drugs and alcohol. After overcoming his bad habits, Carl used his second chance at life to return to a deep commitment to his Christian faith.

As Perkins used Cash's show to put his life back on track, he got to know Maybelle Carter and her daughters. This new version of the Carter Family was now backing Cash on stage. One night while waiting in his dressing room, Perkins began to play around with a new song built on a Carter gospel classic. When the song was completed, Johnny Cash was so impressed he earmarked it for his next recording session.

"Daddy Sang Bass" borrowed a theme from the Carter classic by asking the question, "Will the circle be unbroken, by and by, Lord, by and by?" This new song based on the old standard stayed on the top of the country charts for six weeks.

The next group that revived "Circle" was a part of the acid-rock music scene of the late sixties. The Nitty Gritty Dirt Band had already produced a number of top pop hits when they traveled to Nashville and teamed with Roy Acuff, Doc Watson, Earl Scruggs, Merle Travis, and Maybelle Carter for their new album. The cuts from this double disk set reawakened both the public and the industry to the genre's rich living history and some of its most important older contributors. They also made "Can the Circle Be Unbroken?" the best-known country-gospel song of all time.

The Grammy-winning Nitty Gritty Dirt Band record album took its name from the Carter's old gospel classic. The cut was retitled "Will the Circle Be Unbroken?" but that was about all that had changed. Almost twelve years after A.P.'s death, Maybelle Carter again played the autoharp and sang the lead as more than forty other stars joined in. Although he wasn't there to see it, in a very real way the circle that A.P had hoped would be completed was, and in the process the deep bond between gospel, folk, and country music was reaffirmed.

Child of the King

Some people are called by God to compose inspirational songs, and when they are, the business of putting down the emotions, passions, and truths of gospel lyrics consumes all their writings. All that they write becomes the outward expression of their faith.

Hymn books are filled with the mighty words of men and women who fit into this "called" category. Yet the writing of inspired songs is not limited to those who have been chosen for full-time Christian musical service. Indeed, some of the very best expressions of Christian faith have come from writers who have been inspired just a few times to use their pens to record their spiritual beliefs.

While Cindy Walker may not have been called to write solely gospel songs, she certainly was put on this earth to use her God-given talent to write and compose unforgettable music. The daughter of a salesman, the granddaughter of a minister who composed "Hold to God's Unchanging Hand," and born in a small Depression-era Texas town, Cindy grew up singing, playing guitar, and looking for an audience. By the time she was seven she was not only starring in a Fort Worth stage show, but she was also writing the music for the production. She was a small girl, but she had big dreams. By her teens, this veteran of her own radio show thought she was seasoned enough to sell her wares to music's most famous voices.

In 1941 Cindy eagerly welcomed an opportunity to journey to California with her parents. For her father it was a business trip, for her mother a vacation, for the teenager it was the opportunity of a lifetime. Striding confidently into the Crosby building, with no appointment or introduction, Cindy not only talked her way into Bing Crosby's brother's office, but astonished him with her music. A day later she was playing for Bing himself. Within months he had taken Cindy's "Lone Star Trail" to the top of the charts.

Sensing that their daughter's dreams might indeed become reality, the Walkers moved from Texas to California, where Cindy quickly established herself as the queen of the Western songwriters. In an era when cowboy movies ruled the box office, Walker wrote scores of hits for the likes of Tex Ritter, Gene Autry, Bob Wills, and Eddy Arnold. Almost every singing cowboy movie contained one of her songs. Before she was old enough to vote she owned a large portion of the hit parade. Although she was often able to write twenty songs a week, by 1944 she could not keep up with the demand for her tunes. By the end of World War II more than fifty artists representing every major musical genre had recorded at least one of her songs. More remarkable than the volume of her work was the fact that her treasure chest of self-penned material ran the gamut from pop to big band, from Western swing to folk to country. She could write it all, and it seemed that everything she wrote had "hit" stamped all over it.

In the fifties, tired of the fast pace of Los Angeles life, Cindy moved back to Texas. Still, it didn't matter where she lived, she continued to write. Over the course of the next four decades she composed hits for Ray Charles, Roy Orbison, Elvis Presley, Pat Boone, Dean Martin, Sammy Kaye, Margaret Whiting, Al Dexter, Red Foley, Charlie Daniels, Tennessee Ernie Ford, Hank Snow, Webb Pierce, Billy Walker, Jim Reeves, George Morgan, Gladys Knight and the Pips, and a host of others. More than five hundred of her compositions found their way into recording studios, and scores of them topped the charts.

With a résumé that included such hits as "Cherokee Maiden," "Dusty Skies," "Silver Spurs," "Oklahoma Hills," "You Don't Know Me," "Sugar Moon," "China Doll," "Dream Baby," "In the Misty Moonlight," and "Distant Drums," it is little wonder that Country Music Hall of Fame Songwriter Harlan Howard has called Cindy the greatest living songwriter of country music. It is also little wonder that she has won more awards than the best-known tunesmiths in history. Yet if you were to somehow wrangle a visit to this publicity-shy woman's modest home in Mexia, Texas, you would find no awards, no citations, no autographed pictures or framed gold records hanging on the wall. Even though the industry that her music has so dominated thinks of her as legend, Cindy simply goes about her life much like every other member of the local Presbyterian church she attends each week. No frills, no ego, no display of vestiges of fame, just Sister Walker talking of small-town life, new babies, sick friends, and church needs.

Although she found fame and fortune in secular music, it never turned her head. It also didn't threaten the strong moral fiber that had been implanted in her by her parents. Not so much a tribute to her parents as a statement of her own faith, Cindy took time out to compose a book of hymns at the very time she was ruling the hit parades. "Of Thee We Sing" was made up of original songs based on her own very personal and quiet faith. Simple and direct, these songs, though not chart-toppers, seemed to best reflect the image of the Cindy Walker who walked the streets and attended church in Mexia.

Several of Cindy's gospel efforts found their way to recording studios. One, "Child of the King," was even cut several times in the early fifties. George Younce, a founding member of the legendary Cathedral Quartet, remembers coming across it on an old "78" he found in his attic about 1960:

> I don't remember who had cut it, don't even know why I had put it on the turntable, but when I heard "Child of the King," I was completely captured by the music and the message. Never before had a song so clearly stated to me what my special relationship with my Heavenly Father really was. I was a member of the Blue Ridge Quartet then, so I took the record to them. We not only cut and scored a hit with it, but we sang it at the National Quartet Convention. Not long after it became kind of a quartet standard that everybody did.*

When George left the Blue Ridge Quartet to join the Cathedrals, he brought "Child of the King" with him. Soon Cindy Walker's statement of the royal benefits of being saved became strongly identified with the Cathedral Quartet. They couldn't do a show without including it.

Not even Cindy knows just what inspired her to compose such a strong statement of faith. She says it just came to her. In truth, "Child of the King" is probably the result of a life spent living in a manner that pleased God even while working in a business that often embraced more worldly things. Thus Cindy's example, her faith, and her quiet and humble spirit have not only touched and inspired millions through her songs, but they have also had a profound effect on those who have had the privilege of knowing this modest woman as a real person. Even though she has been ushered into prominent and prestigious places, even though she has been honored by the entertainment industry's most well-known people, and even

---

*Personal interview with George Younce.

though she has been acclaimed as a legend, Cindy Walker has never forgotten that when she accepted Christ she became a child of the King. And when one is a child of royalty, then one has to hold herself or himself to a higher standard than others. Cindy not only said it best in her song but also has lived this truth throughout her remarkable life.

Clinging to a Saving Hand

There has always been a strong tie between country and gospel music. The genres can both trace their roots to the rural South, and many times their lyrics embrace themes of hardship, heartache, and faith. Since the dawning of radio, numerous gospel songs have swept onto country play lists. "Keep on the Sunnyside" and country classics such as "There Goes My Everything" have been rewritten into gospel music classics. The marriage between country and gospel is so deep that it should come as no surprise that many classic gospel songs were born out of the experiences of country songwriters.

In his more than four decades of broadcasting, Bill Mack, country music's most celebrated late-night disc jockey, has helped country and gospel bond together in a very special way. For more than two decades Bill's *Country Crossroads* syndicated radio program has taken the message of Christ and salvation to the airwaves through interviews with many of the top country music stars. With Bill's deep voice asking the questions, country artists such as Barbara Mandrell, Connie Smith, and Minnie Pearl have talked about their faith and how it led them through the good and bad times. There can be little doubt that with Mack at the helm *Country Crossroads* has used country music as a guiding force in saving countless lost souls.

Through his work on *Country Crossroads* and at WBAP in Fort Worth, Bill Mack has become a personality known to millions. His comfortable hosting style has kept many a listener company on long, lonely nights. If Bill, a member of the Disc Jockey Hall of Fame, had done nothing but lend his voice to his nightly radio show and *Country Crossroads*, he would still have become one of country music's most potent personalities. Yet rather than stop there, he has constantly sought to expand his talent and his reach through new avenues and ventures.

One night in the early sixties Mack began to play with an idea for a song. This was nothing unusual; he had been writing for years and some of the top names in the business had recorded his tunes. That night he scratched down the words to what he knew would be a hit for country music's hottest voice, Patsy Cline. But before Bill could mail a demo recording of his "Blue" to Patsy's producer, Owen Bradley, Patsy died in a plane crash. Although he continued to write new material, the demo Bill had crafted just for Cline's magnificent voice was retired.

Seven years later, just as Bill had completed his midnight radio shift at five in the morning, he sat down to try to finish another new song. It was a chore that should have been so easy, most of the work had been done, but he couldn't find an ending. It was the only time in his life that he was at the mercy of his work. For weeks this piece of unfinished business had haunted him and kept him awake. In order to preserve his own peace of mind he knew he couldn't let this work linger undone anymore. He vowed this was the day he was going to put the final words on paper and walk away.

"I went into the WBAP's production room," Mack recalled. "I was determined to finish a song called, 'Take Me From the Shadows of the Trees.' The song was about an atheist who was dying. I had already written most of the lyrics, and the emotions they conveyed were painful and hopeless. I had written a verse that went, 'Don't send me any red or yellow roses. I don't ask for your prayers on bended knees. Don't bury a Bible with my body, I beg you, just take me from the shadows of the trees.'"

It was strange for a strong Christian like Bill to be struggling to compose a song about the emotions of an atheist facing death, yet there was little doubt the lyrics somehow led to Mack's own feelings of hopelessness. The song was a message he didn't like and something he couldn't believe. As he looked for answers, Bill stared out into a cold, pounding rain and the darkness of the hour just before dawn. *Dear God,* he prayed, *I need some help.*

"When I listened to my lyrics," he recalled, "I felt a chill go down my spine. Suddenly, in a way I couldn't explain, I also found that new lyrics had somehow come into my mind. I didn't write them down, they just floated in, but they were so striking that I couldn't forget them."

Using the same tune, Bill changed the message of the song from a hopeless, empty view of death to a Christian's exclamation of faith. The first words he wrote down lifted the clouds that had been haunting his work.

Unlike "Shadows of the Trees," which had remained undone for weeks, "Clinging to a Saving Hand" was completed in just a few moments. As Bill put the finishing touches on the lyrics, the cold rain stopped, dawn broke through the clouds, and the depression that had been hovering over his life lifted. It was as if he had been reborn.

A few weeks later Bill flew to Nashville to cut a demo of "Clinging." The song had become so ingrained in his mind that he didn't even bring a copy of the lyrics, he simply sang them from memory. With demo in hand, the disc jockey personally took the recording to one of country's hottest female singers of the time, Connie Smith. When Connie, whose Christian faith had seen a series of trials and tribulations, listened to "Clinging to a Saving Hand" for the first time, she was convinced that she was hearing her own testimony. She cut the song at her next recording session. Others who quickly adopted "Clinging" as their own included Conway Twitty and Bill Monroe. Soon Bill Mack's inspired vision of eternal hope in the face of death was a regular gospel feature at scores of country music concerts.

Although he had written hits for many other stars, "Clinging to a Saving Hand" quickly become Bill's favorite composition. Using his all-night, clear-channel radio show as his forum, he was able to share his own faith and optimism about a risen Savior by signing off every night with Connie's version of his song. Through letters, phone calls, and cards, the "Midnight Cowboy," as he had been christened by the millions of truckers who tuned in to his show each night, discovered "Clinging" had become an instrument in leading scores of lost and hopeless men and women to Christ.

"I don't feel like I really wrote 'Clinging,'" Bill explained. "It was given to me. I couldn't have come up with the lyrics, 'Sing me a song of praise and glory, help this wand'ring child to understand; that when I close my eyes in sleep eternal, I'll be clinging to a saving hand.' God gave me those words."

Unlike many country-gospel classics, "Clinging to a Saving Hand" wasn't immediately used in church worship services. With its blatantly country tune, this song cried out for twanging fiddles and a steel guitar. "Clinging" just didn't seem to work as well with only a piano for accompaniment. Yet this may have made this song an even stronger tool for Christian outreach. Those who requested "Clinging" usually listened to their music at bars and honky-tonks and never darkened the doors of a church. Through name country acts, as well as local bands, "Clinging to a Saving Hand" offered the message of salvation to those trapped in a neon world of booze and heartache. For the last thirty years thousands of men and women have looked through the smoke, listened to the lyrics, and come home to Christ.

More than two decades after writing "Clinging," Bill Mack attended a Texas Rangers baseball game, where he heard an eleven-year-old girl sing "The Star Spangled Banner." He was so impressed with the young woman's voice that he dusted off the demo of the song he had written for Patsy Cline and sent it to her. Two years later LeeAnn Rimes became a teenage sensation by recording Bill Mack's "Blue." The single and album became #1 in both popular and country music and paved the way for one of the most remarkable careers in modern music history.

Yet as pleased as Bill Mack was that LeeAnn Rimes took "Blue" to the top of the charts, he was much more ecstatic when she chose "Clinging to a Saving Hand" to anchor her first inspirational album. The album "You Light Up My Life" brought the message of faith to millions as it not only became one of 1997's most-played inspirational releases but topped both the pop and country charts as well.

Someday, when Bill Mack dies, "Clinging to a Saving Hand" will be sung at his funeral. Of course, he won't be there to hear it; he will have already awakened at his Savior's feet. And thanks to the message of the song that began as an atheist's dark and hopeless plea, Bill will be joined by many others who saw the hope and light through the lyrics of "Clinging to a Saving Hand."

Crying in the Chapel

Crying in the Chapel," the song that produced a Grammy and a gold record for Elvis Presley in 1960, has never really been thought of as a gospel classic but rather as a rock-and-roll or rhythm-and-blues standard. Because the song first landed on the pop charts, because it was a standard concert pick for many of the black and country groups of the mid-fifties, and because it was never a favorite of choirs and church congregations, "Crying in the Chapel" has never received its due as an inspirational classic and as an important link in the connection between gospel and rock music.

Every major music historian traces rock and country music to their roots in both black blues and gospel, but only a few within gospel circles recognize that it's a two-way street. Gospel music has also been influenced by what was happening in country and rock. Songs such as "Satisfied" and "Happy Rhythm" owe their message to faith, but they owe their beat to the secular hit parades of the time. The message of "Crying in the Chapel" was definitely born of a church experience, but the song first found favor on charts that normally rejected gospel music out of hand.

"Crying in the Chapel" was written in 1953 by Artie Glenn. Glenn was a Fort Worth, Texas, factory line worker at an aircraft plant when he was stricken with a serious back problem. A guitar player who once toured with Bob Wills, he knew firsthand the hard life of country music's tours. One-night stands and smoky honky-tonks were much more familiar to him than all-day singings and Sunday school picnics. Still, during his youth he had spent many hours listening to fire-and-brimstone sermons on hard wooden pews on hot summer days. So when he fell ill, he fully understood the consequences of sin and the meaning of repentance.

Lying in a hospital bed, about to undergo spinal surgery with its tremendous risks, Glenn again grasped at the religion of his youth. Praying hard and long, often with tears in his eyes, he promised he would change his ways if the Lord would allow him to walk out of the hospital. He vowed to rededicate his life to the Lord, if God would somehow help the surgeons heal his back.

When his prayers were answered, Glenn remembered the vow that he had made. As soon as he was released from Harris Hospital, he refused to go home to his wife and children until he found a church in which he could say a prayer of thanks and offer his life to the Lord. The first chapel he discovered was Loving Avenue Baptist Church—a modest structure built from the lumber of a long-since-forgotten mule barn. Rushing through the open doors and falling to his knees, he lowered his head and wept for several minutes.

As Glenn walked out of the chapel, he reflected on the miracle of his surgery and the joy he had felt while praying in the chapel. By the time he found his way to his house, he had already written a simple tune and a chorus that would lay the foundation for his own musical testimony.

After completing the chorus and singing it to himself several times, Glenn quickly finished the remainder of his song. He then played his musical testimony for his younger brother Darrell, who was just a teenager at the time. Artie wanted to share his newfound message of hope, as well as the miracle of his cure and redemption. Darrell not only took the song and message to heart, but sought out a way to get "Crying in the Chapel" professionally recorded. Using a local studio, he cut a demo of his brother's song. Released by a local label in the summer of 1953, Darrell's demo recording miraculously landed on the national charts, climbing into *Billboard's* top ten. Fueled by the single's success, a host of other artists raced out to cover the song, including June Valli, Ella Fitzgerald, Art Lund, and the R&B group—the Orioles. With Sonny Till singing the lead, the Orioles' version of "Crying in the Chapel" became a best seller and was certified as pure gold. Rex Allen also cut a country gospel version of "Crying in the Chapel" that was closer to the original Glenn concept than any of the other popular versions. But it was through the Orioles that the song written by a former country musician in a small Texas Baptist church would soon be hailed as one of rock and roll's first major hits.

For the next seven years "Crying in the Chapel" was viewed as an R&B standard and dismissed in both black and white gospel circles. Artie Glenn's song about answered prayer and redemption might have remained buried in rock-and-roll history if Elvis Presley hadn't decided to cut it in 1960.

Elvis, who had been raised with both black and white gospel influences, was enamored with "Crying in the Chapel," thanks to the Orioles' rendition. Using their styling, he cut a recording that was placed on his second gospel album, "How Great Thou Art." Not only did "Chapel" help win Presley his first Grammy, but it also proved so successful that it was released as an RCA single six years later. Even in the face of the British musical invasion and the beginnings of acid rock, it landed in rock chart's top five. Not only was it Presley's first hit in years, but it also began a wave of rock successes that embraced gospel themes. The best remembered of these is Judy Collins' version of "Amazing Grace."

More than two dozen acts eventually added "Crying in the Chapel" to their recording repertoire, though none scored as highly as Presley. In 1997 the Orioles' version of Glenn's song was revived when it was used for the soundtrack of Sean Connery's movie *Just Cause.*

Artie Glenn never scored with another hit, yet his one hit song serves as a reminder not only that the message of salvation can be welcomed into almost every musical format but also that the line between popular recording and gospel music is not as great as most people imagine. More importantly, "Crying in the Chapel" also serves as a testimony to a forgiving Lord who reaches out to all who come to Him.

Everybody Will Be Happy

*E*ugene Monroe Bartlett was probably one of the most optimistic men ever to walk on the earth. Even when everyone else was carrying an umbrella to keep dry, it seemed that he saw very little but rainbows and sunny skies. Not only did he relish each day of his life, but he made every attempt to bring others up to his level of optimism. While he recognized suffering and loss and saw and felt others' pain, he didn't let it cloud his own joy in knowing Christ and walking each day with Him. Long before Norman Vincent Peale wrote *The Power of Positive Thinking*, Bartlett was living it.

For much of his adult life Bartlett roamed the country teaching at singing schools and conventions, giving special concerts, and meeting with up-and-coming songwriters. Although it often kept him from his family and the Arkansas Ozark Mountains' home he dearly loved, Bartlett always seemed to have the time to visit with anyone who sought him out. The testimonies of those who were touched by his quick smile and warm words would fill several books. Yet being an "Ambassador of Sunshine" was just a small part of his life.

There can be little doubt that Bartlett's publishing concern, the Hartford Music Company, had a great deal to do with the rapid spread of gospel music between 1920 and World War II. Not only did he write scores of inspirational songs for these books, he also discovered and published a host of new writers, including Albert E. Brumley.

To enhance the impact of his company's music, as well as drum up even more publicity for his concerts and singing schools, Bartlett founded a magazine, *Herald of Song*, which centered on the world of gospel music. Read by thousands each month, this publication was a pioneer in using music to reach lost souls.

Bartlett's earthly fame was assured when he wrote "Victory in Jesus." The song became a standard in hundreds of hymnals, a choral favorite, and a musical testimony for thousands of Christians. Yet while "Victory" and scores of other great hymns had made Bartlett a dynamic force in gospel music, his positive outlook and whimsical humor were often used in secular writings too.

Grand Ole Opry star Little Jimmie Dickens made a huge hit with Bartlett's "Take an Old Cold Tater and Wait." Along with self-penned numbers such as "You Can't Keep a Good Man Down," "The Old Razor Strop," and "The Men Will Never Wear Kimonos By and By," Bartlett's songs brought giggles and smiles to crowds who had come especially to hear his religious music. Bartlett had always felt that laughter was an important part of the spiritual healing most people needed. He lived by the principle that a Christian who had truly embraced the message of salvation was indeed a happy person.

The spirit of E.M. Bartlett can probably best be seen in his classic gospel song "Everybody Will Be Happy Over There." Every word, every phrase, and every beat of this up-tempo, quartet-driven number portrays the joy not only of heaven but also of living a Christian life on earth.

For a songwriter such as Bartlett, the task of writing "Everybody Will Be Happy Over There" was easy. The song was a statement of his personal beliefs; therefore each verse naturally flowed into the next, and the song's tempo echoed many of the great convention standards that were so prevalent in the decade before World War II. The bass lead in the chorus was typical of not only what congregations wanted but also what was popular with quartets on the radio. With words and a melody that are easy to remember and a harmony elementary in design, all anchored to a joyous optimism attained only through faith, "Everybody Will Be Happy Over There" is a classic example of what made southern gospel music quickly become so popular. Yet these simply defined elements of the song are also the reason it is so easy to overlook the real genius that went into it.

Bartlett spent his life trying to make people feel better by giving them tonic for their souls. Rather than using fire and brimstone to scare them into salvation, he took a New Testament approach and presented the real joy of serving the Lord. Bartlett knew this joy was infectious when expressed in song. Anyone who has ever sung one of his songs knows they all end with a smile.

Bartlett wore a smile through bad times as well as good. When felled by a stroke, when his voice was silenced and his hands were made useless, when his world suddenly was whittled down to a single room, he still managed a daily smile. When asked how he could stay so positive, he would grin and explain that there was joy in his heart because he knew the truth of the song "Everybody Will Be Happy Over There."

Farther Along

In the minds of those who listen to their sermons and seek their counsel, preachers are the men with all the answers. They can find just the right words to comfort a sick parishioner, bring solace to a mourning family, or lead a doubting soul to Christ. Yet what is so often forgotten in listening to the wise and prayerful words that come from the mouths of pastors is that they are human too. They suffer the same pains, temptations, doubts, fears, and heartaches as do the members of their congregations.

W.B. Stevens was one of those who seemed to have all the answers. He was a small-town preacher whose flock in Queen City, Missouri, looked to him as a beacon. Even in a world changing as rapidly as America was in 1900, he seemed to always know the answers to life's hard questions. Grounded in fundamental biblical study, Reverend Stevens stood for what was right, and it seemed because he had lived so righteously, his life was blessed. He had a loving wife, a wonderful son, and the respect of those around him.

For hundreds of years progress in America had moved at a snail's pace, a revolutionary invention coming only about once in a lifetime. For as long as folks could remember, the horse had been the primary means of transportation, candles had lit up the night, and letters had been the sole way of connecting with a friend or loved one in another place. But now people were building cars, electricity was finding its way even into rural homes, and the telephone was becoming more than a novelty. With pictures moving on large screens, people talking of flying, and adding machines making laborious chores seem easy, America was evolving at a pace that not only frightened many people but also made them question long-held, accepted beliefs. This change was seen by many as the Devil's work, and some who had once been a part of God's flock now seemed to worship man's latest inventions more than they did the Lord. Unlike many, the Reverend Stevens was not fearful of the future. Not only did he not fear it, he saw changes as opportunities to advance the kingdom of God, and he couldn't wait to share these opportunities with his son.

In many ways the relationship between a father and his son was more special then. In those slower times, there were moments when quiet conversation allowed for exchanges that rarely exist in today's world so crowded by television, radio, and computers. Even though progress seemed to be moving at the speed of light, in the early 1900s there was still plenty of time for fishing, picnics, and sitting in porch swings. There was still time to dream of what lay ahead for a boy with so much potential.

In an imperfect world, dreams often have a way of turning into nightmares. Such was the case for Stevens. His son died suddenly while he was still very young, before his father could even say good-bye. Suddenly the minister who knew all the right words to comfort others could not find any for himself.

For a while Stevens was less a pastor than a struggling parent. Overcome with grief, he realized that nothing anyone said offered him the peace he sought. Saddened beyond measure, consumed with his loss, he found it a brutal fight just to make his way out into the world each day. In his own mind his sermons rang hollow and his statements of faith seemed grounded more in memorized Bible verses than in real-life experience.

Perhaps it was because he was used to writing down his thoughts into his sermons that Reverend Stevens began to scribble down his own mournful feelings of inadequacy. The rough lines written on tear-stained paper were his way of trying to communicate not only with God but also with himself:

"Why is it that the people who live for God seem to suffer more than those who ignore his commandments?"

"Does God think that suffering will make us better and stronger?"

"How could God let such painful things happen?"

"What hope is there in a life where the good are not rewarded for their faithfulness?"

As these questions stared back at him and as he looked out his window and saw people who were living in sin while also living in luxury, he must have wondered if there were any rewards for living a Christian life. He also must have questioned his own calling to the ministry.

In the pain of the moment Stevens composed a musical sermon that spoke not only to him in his grief but also to anyone who had ever wanted to ask God, "Why me?"

Taken by itself, the first stanza of "Farther Along" is a hopeless prayer of a faithless man. Because the words dwell on death and on life's unfairness, it seems to renounce faith in a just God. Yet Stevens didn't stop there. In the song's final two stanzas "Farther Along" rings out strong as a testament of faith. In trying to answer his own grief, Stevens grew to know he was not wise enough to begin to understand God's plan. Yet through his Bible study and his prayers, he also realized that one day, when he and his son would be reunited, he would be given the answers that haunted him as he mourned. His faith to wait until that time did more than help him grow past his heartache: its expression in song has inspired thousands of others to keep the faith in even the darkest times. Given time, everything will be explained.

"Farther Along," revealing a father's heartache to the world, has become one of the best-known Christian songs dealing with the unanswered questions of life. Recorded countless times and sung in thousands of churches during hundreds of thousands of services, its personal message of faith in a world that provides few answers makes "Farther Along" not only one of the first true gospel songs but also one of the most beloved.

Give the World a Smile

When Marion Snider was a small boy, many farm families were still plowing with mules and riding horse-drawn carts to church. Radio was a new invention, and motion pictures were silent. It was a time for invention, innovation, and imagination. Thanks to a lot of God-given ability and a great deal of hard work, Snider was able to witness firsthand that era's spirit of creation and to participate in it as well.

"When I was a young boy, still wearing knee britches and riding a Shetland pony," Snider remembered, "I went to singing schools. Gospel music had always been a part of my life. When I was twelve I had a very special experience. Otis Deaton and M.L. Yandell came to our town and taught a school that lasted two weeks. One of the songs they taught us was a thing they had written called 'Give the World a Smile.' Little did I realize then that I would later have the opportunity to help introduce this song to the world."

By the late twenties radio had opened up gospel music to millions and allowed songwriters such as Deaton and Yandell to finally gain exposure for their work. Radio opened the door to a world of opportunity for Snider also.

"I went to the Stamps-Baxter singing school in 1933 in midwinter normal [session]," Snider explained. "From there I began working theaters playing piano. Then I met the Lubbock Quartet. They wanted me to play some of their concerts in East Texas. I did, and we had enough success that I returned to Lubbock and enrolled at Texas Tech. After a while I decided there was a bit too much sand in West Texas and returned home. Yet I couldn't stay away for long. I went back to Tech in 1935. I was sitting under a tree on the campus when I got a telegram from V.O. Stamps of the Stamps-Baxter Company. He had wired to ask me to play piano for the Stamps Quartet. It was an offer I couldn't refuse."

For the next four years Marion Snider played the piano for the world's most famous Christian quartet. On the road, on their daily KRLD radio show, at the singing school, and on records, it was the young Texan who set the mood and pace with his jazz-styled playing. In short order he became as much of the identity of the Stamps as any of the quartet's singers. There can be little doubt that his "between the keys" style of playing (hitting notes that no one else could find) influenced almost every gospel pianist that came after him.

"Early in my days with the Stamps," Snider remembered, "I went into the studio. V.O. had a song that he wanted us to do for the Texas Centennial program." As he sat down at the piano, he saw two very familiar names on the top of his sheet music—Otis Deaton and M.L. Yandell. He was about to play the song he had learned as a child.

"I started; then the quartet joined in on the after beat," he recalled. "It sounded just as great then as it does today. After we finished, V.O. announced, 'This song is going to be our theme song. People are going to hear it worldwide.' He was right, too."

"Give the World a Smile" created a sensation the first time the Stamps sang it on radio. Then, almost overnight, the bass-driven number became gospel music's most recognized theme song. Not only did the original Stamps Quartet use it daily, but almost every one of the hundreds of regional Stamps Quartet groups also opened their radio shows and concerts with it.

Other quartets, such as the Blackwood Brothers, quickly picked it up as well. By 1940 it could already be found in scores of hymnals.

A part of the joy of "Give the World a Smile" came from its upbeat piano lead and wonderful four-part voice blend. Yet beyond the beat and harmony, Deaton and Yandell had penned a wonderful message within the lyrics as well.

"I think that 'Give the World a Smile' presents the greatest sermon you will ever hear in a song," Snider explained. "Think about those words! 'Give the world a smile every day, helping someone on life's dreary way,' beginning and ending with 'the joy of serving Jesus with a smile.' In those verses are incredible words. This is a message we should all take to heart. I think that is why 'Give the World a Smile' has become the theme song of every gospel music singer in the universe."

Marion Snider played "Give the World a Smile" every day for four years. He never grew tired of it. In 1940, after his mentor V.O. Stamps died, he moved to Washington, D.C., and CBS radio with the Rangers Quartet. He took the song with him. During World War II, when he served in the Navy as a chaplain, he made sure that tens of thousands of servicemen left for the battlefields with Deacon and Yandell's words on their lips. For three and a half years he began and ended most of his services with "Give the World a Smile."

After the war Snider returned to civilian life and formed his own quartet. Based in Dallas and sponsored by a sugar company, the Imperials became one of the best-known southern gospel groups in history. Over the course of the next decade they not only headed up their own Texas Radio Network program but also worked with Eddy Arnold, Minnie Pearl, Little Jimmie Dickens, and Ethel Waters. "Smile" was a part of their show, too. In the fifties, when Snider finally cut back on his schedule to spend more time with his family, he turned the Imperials over to Jake Hess. Hess kept the spirit and message of the song alive even after Snider left.

Today Marion Snider is in his eighties, yet age has not slowed him down. Several times a week he still mounts a stage and sits down at a piano. With his hands on the keyboard, he pauses for a moment, then hits a familiar introduction that brings a smile to every face in the audience, including his own. Before he finishes "Give the World a Smile" everyone is singing along with him—the man who was there when it was introduced to the world.

For much of their lives Otis Deaton and M.L. Yandell thought they knew the power of a song. For many years they believed so much in that power that they traveled throughout the South teaching others how to read music and sing. Yet at no time could they ever have guessed that one of their students would help take one of their songs to the whole world and that this song would become the identifying symbol of southern gospel music itself. "Give the World a Smile" proved the power of a song, but, more than that, it proved the power of God to use that song to reach millions generation after generation. From an era of invention, imagination, and innovation, this song remains the perfect blend of all three.

Glory Train

$\mathcal{A}$ quick glance through an old Stamps-Baxter songbook reveals that many of the top songwriters of the era worked trains into their verses. To most people who heard these tunes during the Depression, it seemed only natural that a train would carry a person's soul to a better place. After all, trains carried people and their belongings everywhere.

In the years after World War II, a time when the nation's highways improved and a robust economy allowed almost every American to own a car, the romance of the rails began to die. As diesel-powered locomotives replaced the old steam engines, engineers ceased to be icons, and children began to dream of landing on the moon or taking a spaceship to Mars. Even in country music, where the "Wabash Cannonball" and "The Orange Blossom Special" had long been considered anthems, train songs were being pushed off the charts by stories of truck drivers and hot rods.

In the late fifties, at about the same time the Russians jump-started the space race by launching a dog into orbit, George Younce was singing bass with the Blue Ridge Quartet. On a night off, he joined his family for an evening of television. One of the shows that flashed its black-and-white images into the Younce living room was *The Adventures of Ozzie and Harriet*.

"I was just sitting there watching the show," Younce remembered, "and at the end of the episode Ricky Nelson was singing to an audience of both kids and adults. This was the show's normal format, as they usually had Ricky introduce his latest single in this way. On this night he did something different. He didn't perform a new rock-and-roll song or an old hit; rather, he and his band sang a gospel song I had never heard before."

By the end of the first verse Younce was humming along with Ricky Nelson on "Glory Train." The next day he informed the members of the Blue Ridge Quartet that he just discovered their next single release. As it turned out, they became only the first of many gospel groups to put their stamp on it.

Ricky Nelson's version of "Glory Train" offered many rock-and-roll fans their first exposure to pure gospel music. In a very real sense, contemporary Christian music may have begun with this effort. Yet "Glory Train" and the teenage idol would never have come together if an Alabama country band hadn't fallen on hard times.

Thomas Baker Knight had just finished a tour of duty in the service when he found a day job working at a Birmingham, Alabama, factory and a night gig playing with a country music band. From the money he was making on both jobs, he was able to buy a car, rent an apartment, and put some new strings on his guitar. In the young man's view, life looked good. When his band received an offer to play for some record scouts in Nashville, things looked even brighter. Yet in Music City about the only person Knight and his boys impressed was a songwriter. She thought his original tunes showed some merit, but she didn't have enough power to get him a job. Discouraged, he soon watched his band break up around him. At about the same time, he lost his job at the factory. Within weeks he was out of money, his car had been repossessed, and he was just days from getting kicked out of his apartment. Unable to find work, Knight was beginning to wonder where he was going to live and how he was going to eat come the first of the next month.

"I got a call from an old buddy in Los Angeles," Knight recalled. "He told me about a job as an extra in a motion picture. He sent me the money for a plane ticket. I packed my clothes and guitar and headed west. When I got there the job only lasted a day. Within just a few weeks I was facing the same bleak future I had in Alabama. I had no work and no prospects."

After a day spent hitting the streets looking for a job, he returned to his cheap apartment. Pulling an old jar off a shelf, he twisted off the lid and poured his life savings onto a table. He counted the change three times. Each time the final total was thirty-eight cents.

"That was all I had," he recalled. "I didn't know how I was going to eat, pay the rent, or anything. I had pretty much given up when I heard a knock at the door. When I opened it, I came face to face with Ricky Nelson."

The songwriter Knight had impressed in Nashville had seen him in Los Angeles a few days later. When she talked with Nelson, she told the rock idol where Knight was and that he might have some songs Nelson could use for his next recording session. Following up on the lead, the nation's favorite teenage rocker decided to see what Knight had written.

"I played a couple of things for him," Knight remembered. "He listened, thanked me, and left. I didn't think I had impressed him and figured I had blown my last chance in the business. Yet a few hours later Ricky's agent came to my door. He wanted to discuss a writing contract."

As Knight glanced at the jar that was partially filled with pennies, Nelson's agent offered him a $2,000 advance if he would sign with their publishing company. The starving writer didn't argue. A few weeks later Nelson recorded Knight's "Lonesome Town," and Knight was suddenly a very hot commodity. Over the course of the next few months the singer and the songwriter scored several more impressive rock hits. This string of hits and Nelson's interest in reaching new markets with something special motivated them to try something new.

"Ricky had really been impressed with the gospel music Elvis had recorded," Knight recalled. "He was already using a gospel quartet, the Jordanaires, on his sessions. He loved the music they sang, so he decided he wanted to cut some spiritual music too. Yet he didn't want to do anything traditional. He wanted me to write something original for him.

"I had a strong church background, so I thought about the songs I had grown up singing in church. When I took myself back in time to my musical roots, the spirit and inspiration came easily."

An old train that had often passed by his church offered Knight a theme that seemed perfect for his initial effort. Yet instead of riding this train to Memphis, he rode it to Glory. After a bit of polishing, he took it to Ricky. With producer Jimmy Haskell setting the arrangement, Nelson not only cut this new gospel song, but aimed it at the rock market. Although James Burton—who would grow into one of rock's most honored guitar players—laid down some solid rock-and-roll lead work, the Jordanaires provided the standard back-up vocals, and the rest of Nelson's band stayed with a rock-and-roll beat, Nelson's straightforward singing of the lyrics left the message intact. This was still a gospel song!

Any of the millions of viewers who listened to "Glory Train" that night must have been surprised. It was rock and roll all right, but with a Christian theme. The song talked about Jesus, salvation, and heaven. Even when Elvis had cut his gospel songs, he hadn't done it this way. Critics wondered if Ricky's Christian gospel would fly. They questioned if using the beat and guitar wouldn't rally more churches against this youth music than win new fans.

The mere fact that "Glory Train" quickly became one of Nelson's most requested songs reflects not only how well rock/gospel was accepted in 1958 but also how much a marriage of message and beat could mean to many young people. Although contemporary Christian music would not surface for another two decades, this initial rock/gospel classic first illuminated a young market hungry for songs using a rocking rhythm to drive a Christian message.

Ricky Nelson continued to sing occasional gospel songs, including "Glory Train," for the rest of his life. "Glory Train" has grown into a gospel music favorite. The Cathedrals recently put their spin on it. And Thomas Baker Knight, who wrote more than six hundred songs and penned big hits not only for Ricky Nelson but also for Elvis Presley and a host of country acts, now writes music inspired by both the gospel music of his youth and the contemporary gospel sounds his "Glory Train" helped create.

The Gospel Ship

$\mathcal{T}$he Gospel Ship" is an optimistic, upbeat, spiritual anthem of joy. Known and loved by millions, initially identified with the LeFevres and later with the Happy Goodmans and Mylon LeFevre, it has been reworked countless times into country and southern gospel music, a choral anthem, and a rocking spiritual arrangement. In every form this ship has brought happiness to millions for generations, yet almost no one knows where these incredibly optimistic lyrics were born.

> *I have good news to bring and that is why I sing.*
> *All my joys with you I'll share;*
> *I'm going take a trip in the Old Gospel Ship*
> *And go sailing through the air.*

"It was probably the first song I ever learned," remembers Mylon LeFevre. "My mother had probably been singing it all her life too."

As a matter of record, when the song first appeared in songbooks in 1939, Mylon's uncle, Altus LeFevre, was listed as the song's arranger. The Tennessee Music and Printing Company, as well as the Stamps-Baxter Music and Printing Company, actually didn't list a writer. They didn't know who wrote it. Even Altus, who was a student of both African-American and southern gospel music, didn't have a clue as to the song's background. He just knew he had been hearing it for as long as he could remember, and everywhere he went people loved that old song.

"For many years it was our sugar stick," Eva Mae LeFevre recalled. "We would do it real fast and the audience just couldn't get enough of it. Every time we sang it people sprang to their feet. We would often use it when we felt the crowd just wasn't getting into the spirit. No matter how dead they had been, when we started singing 'The Gospel Ship,' they would always come alive."

One of the keys to the LeFevres' version of the old song was tempo. In a lot of the churches of the period, many song leaders would draw "The Gospel Ship" out. Altus LeFevre thought this kind of arrangement ruined the song's emotion. He saw these lyrics as being created by a man who was in love with living, knew the full joy of life on earth, and was filled with the Spirit and anxious to get to heaven. When his family group sang it, he wanted them to convey both the excitement and the joy of homecoming.

O I can scarcely wait, I know I'll not be late,
For I'll spend my time in prayer
And when my ship comes in I will leave this world of sin
And go sailing thru the air.

For almost two decades the LeFevres were so closely identified with "The Gospel Ship" that few other southern gospel groups sang it. Yet in the early sixties not only did another family ensemble begin to put the song into their performances, but by 1973, it had all but become theirs.

"I don't know what urged them to do it," recalled Tanya Goodman Sikes, "but by the early seventies they [The Happy Goodmans] started doing it a lot. I think one of the things that made it so popular with the people who came out to see Dad, Uncle Howard, Aunt Vestal, and Uncle Sam was the way 'The Gospel Ship' was introduced. Vestal had been ill for a while.

The folks who had gotten to love our family missed her very much. Many worried that her heart trouble would keep her from ever singing again. Finally, when she regained her strength, they used 'The Gospel Ship' to kind of welcome her back. My dad and my uncles would sing the song through, then they would leave the stage. They knew that the crowd would always call them back for an encore, so when they came back and started singing 'The Gospel Ship' again, Vestal came back out with them to take the lead."

Using the "The Gospel Ship" as the vehicle to bring Vestal Goodman back to gospel music deeded ownership of the song to The Happy Goodmans for many years. Using a fast, dramatic, spirited arrangement, not unlike that of the LeFevres, the Goodmans reintroduced this solid old vessel at just the moment when southern gospel was exploding. Soon everyone in the business was putting their spin on the song. It became so familiar that a second-generation LeFevre decided to redo it once more, this time for a younger audience:

> *If you're ashamed of me you have no cause to be,*
> *For with Christ I am an heir;*
> *If too much fault you find you will sure be left behind*
> *While I go sailing thru the air.*

"I remember my family singing 'Gospel Ship' on the *Grand Ole Opry*," Mylon LeFevre explained. "I thought it had a mountain flair to it. But as I was in contemporary Christian music, I wanted it to have a rock beat. I rearranged it, and the kids really enjoyed the new arrangement of the old song. Yet this led to a lot of young fans' believing that I had written it. I had to explain that I hadn't and that I didn't know who had. At that point I decided to find out everything I could about the song's origin."

Mylon's quest to discover the roots of the old song led to a professor who had made a study of Negro spirituals. When LeFevre mentioned "The Gospel Ship," the gentleman's eyes lit up.

"The story of the song actually began in Africa," he explained. "Slave traders captured many young natives and chained them together. They were herded onto a ship like cattle. For weeks they were kept in the bow of the ship. If they cried out, they were whipped. Fed very little, placed in quarters so close they couldn't even lie down, many of them died. Their bodies were tossed into the ocean without so much as a prayer. For men who had once lived life running free in their homeland it was a nightmare too disturbing to comprehend. None of them really even understood the word 'slave.'

"One certain young man who survived the trip across the Atlantic only to find himself in a strange new world he had never known existed realized that everything and everyone he loved was now a world away. The United States had been a nation for only a few years. Everything, including the language, was new to him. Frightened, alone, and caged like an animal, the young man was sure that he would soon be killed.

"This slave was sold to a man who worked him with hundreds of other African natives on a large plantation. Over time the young man discovered that he had no hope of freedom. He would never be able to choose what he did or to have a family, a home, or any possessions, and he would not be able to explore the world around him.

"After a few years, he was sold to a new master who introduced the slave to the story of Jesus Christ. Through a church built for the slaves, the young man learned about God. He took the good news of salvation to heart and became a Christian. Although his body was enslaved and although he still had no hope of ever escaping to again run free, he found that his soul had escaped the chains that bound his body.

"When he grew to understand his faith, he used it to help him get through the torture of his existence. Over time he didn't fret about the hopelessness of his own life, and he began to picture a ship in his mind. Yet rather than bring men to a life of slavery and pain, this ship took them to eternal freedom and joy. Setting his thoughts to music, he took his story of 'The Gospel Ship' to the fields with him. He sang it for others, sharing with them the joy that they could find only through Christ."

> *O I'm gonna take a trip, in the good Old Gospel Ship,*
> *I'm going far beyond the sky;*
> *O I'm gonna shout and sing until the heavens ring,*
> *When I'm bidding this world good-bye.*

For two hundred years "The Gospel Ship" has come to mean so much to so many because everyone is a slave to something. Although most of us know more freedom in one day than the song's writer knew in his whole adult life, we are still bound by worldly concerns, temptations, and fears. Knowing God frees us from the pain and suffering of this life by enabling us to see the better days that are just ahead. All Christians, even in the worst of times, should be able to sing, "I have good news to bring!"

The Great Speckled Bird

Even though he died in 1992, Roy Acuff is still widely known as "The King of Country Music." The first living artist ever inducted into the Country Music Association's Hall of Fame, Acuff was bigger than life. A product of a gospel background and steeped in the lore of folk stories and music, this fiddle-playing entertainer represented both the fulfillment of the American dream and the qualities of the American gentleman.

The son of a Baptist minister, he probably would have earned his living in major league baseball if a heat stroke hadn't cut short his playing days. After recovery, Acuff, too weak for manual labor, considered accepting a call to full-time Christian service as a preacher. After much prayer and soul searching, he gave up the notion of filling a pulpit and began to scratch around on one of the family violins. It was with a bow and his father's fiddle that he found his calling, but it would take an old gospel song and a lot of work before he gained any fame or fortune.

In 1931 Roy formed his own band, the Tennessee Cracker-jacks, and worked square dances throughout eastern Tennessee. A year later his band landed a regular spot on Knoxville's noon radio favorite "Mid-Day Merry Go Round." A slip of an announcer's tongue changed the band's name to the Crazy Tennesseans, and it seemed to fit. With no recording contracts and only small-time dates, the group was virtually starving to death. So it seemed crazy to continue to try to make a living in show business. Yet even though a few band members dropped out and had to be replaced, Roy kept playing.

In the early thirties the Carter Family had scored a popular music hit with a folk song called "I'm Thinking Tonight of My Blue Eyes." Roy Acuff was familiar with the song and had used it in his performance. He was shocked when in early 1937 he heard The Black Shirts band sing the same tune with much different words. He was captivated not only by the new lyrics but also by their religious message. He traced the roots of "The Great Speckled Bird" and discovered that the religiously framed story had been written by a minister, Guy Smith. The song's unusual words had been inspired by one of Smith's sermons, which had been based on Jeremiah 12:9: "Mine heritage is unto me as a speckled bird, the birds round about are against her; come ye, assemble all the beasts of the field, come to devour" (KJV).

Acuff was so moved by the song's story of a bird representing Christian faith and soaring to heaven that he decided to learn all six stanzas. Yet he couldn't track down the Reverend Smith, and no one else seemed to know more than just a couple of stanzas of the song. Finally he met singer Charlie Swain. Swain knew all the words and informed Acuff that he would gladly share them with him for a price. Acuff bought the verses for a half dollar.

From the first time he performed it on stage, his crowds went crazy for "The Great Speckled Bird." Those who were dancing stopped and reverently listened to each word as the singer's wailing voice delivered it. As he finished the last line and a Dobro mournfully faded the last instrumental riff, most crowds demanded to hear it again. On some nights Roy and his band played the song as many as six times in a row. Largely because of the song, word got to Nashville's *Grand Ole Opry* that there was a hot band in East Tennessee. Offered an audition for the famed radio show, Acuff and his Tennesseans played "The Great Speckled Bird." Acuff believed this song to be not only his ticket to the big time but also the answer to his prayer. The *Opry* staff jumped on his bandwagon and gave him a spot on the next Saturday night program. When he and his Crazy Tennesseans opened with "The Great Speckled Bird," the audience demanded three encores before the group was allowed to perform another number.

Although Acuff was not aware of it, American Record Company's talent scout and producer William R. Calaway was looking for someone who knew all the words to the song. Calaway had also heard several different versions of it, but none of them seemed complete. When he heard Acuff, he knew he had found what he was looking for.

In 1938 Acuff's "Great Speckled Bird" was released on the Vocation record label. By this time Roy had written four additional stanzas to go with the song's original six. In order to include all ten, the producer put the first five on side one and the other five on what was usually reserved for the "B" side of the record. In retrospect it appeared to have been a very wise move. By the end of the year Roy's first release had climbed to the #10 spot on the pop charts.

"The Great Speckled Bird" made Roy Acuff a star and assured his place in country music, but the song meant a great deal more. Guy Smith's lyrics inspired hope in the time of the Great Depression. Then, during World War II, the song brought tears during every *Opry* broadcast as country music fans took the song to heart as a prayer for their loved ones overseas. The Japanese quickly picked up on what Roy and his special gospel message meant to American soldiers. To try to lure United States troops out from cover, Japanese soldiers were often heard to cry out, "Down with Roosevelt! Down with Babe Ruth! Down with Roy Acuff!"

Roy Acuff was not a gifted singer. In fact his voice was pure country—loud and raw. He was a "hillbilly" and proud of it. He was also humble, a preacher's kid who seemed to have a sermon on his heart that could be released only through the song "The Great Speckled Bird." For these reasons, God-fearing men and women who would have little to do with most country music performers flocked to Roy's shows. Those fans may have cried out for "Wabash Cannonball," but they didn't go home until they had heard "The Great Speckled Bird."

On the wings of a bird Roy had flown to the *Opry* and to fame, and for five decades his personality dominated the mother church of country music. The marriage of country and gospel, which made "The Great Speckled Bird" so much a part of the rural music in the thirties, forties, and fifties, remains important today. The message, which Roy Acuff was able to purchase for fifty cents in 1937, not only inspired millions but helped cement gospel music's place at *The Grand Ole Opry*. This position has helped make Nashville the center of the gospel music world and the *Opry* the home of many of the genre's most important performances.

Happy Rhythm

*L*ong before the term "contemporary Christian music" was invented, long before Amy Grant was even born, and a few years before rock and roll was even identified as a musical genre, Mosie Lister plugged into a sound that pushed the envelope of southern gospel music further than any song that had come before. The tune that was playing in his head in 1953 and the words that were repeating themselves over and over again in his mind drove this former piano tuner to write something unique, something special, and something that represented a new direction in southern gospel music.

"Well, I have been criticized for some of the songs I have written," Lister reflected, "but I think God looks on the heart. In the case of 'Happy Rhythm' I was just having fun. A part of the sound and a part of the things that were said in the song came from some of the black singers I knew. I thought they sang wonderful songs, and I enjoyed their heartfelt styles. I even heard some of the older black folks talk about rocking and rolling in church. I just took that phrase and found that I could easily fit it into a song. That is really how it all came together."

Today no one would hesitate to mix an African-American feel into white southern gospel music. But during the days of the Korean war, a time when baseball was only partially integrated, what Lister was doing was considered revolutionary.

Although begun in fun, "Happy Rhythm" soon took on a life of its own. It really did reflect not only the feel of the African-American gospel musicians who had influenced Lister but also his own positive outlook on Christian life and service. This was a happy man. He was a person who felt great joy every day of his life.

"When I finished it I knew that it was an excellent stage song," Lister recalled. "I also thought it would be a good song for the Statesmen. 'Happy Rhythm' fit their sound and personality. I met with them, and they learned it exactly as I had written it. They got into the words and music easily too. Right after I taught it to them, they were going to a show in a Georgia high school. They introduced it there. When they finished singing it for the first time, people were standing in their seats and shouting."

That first night the crowd wouldn't let Big Chief James S. Wetherington, Hovie Lister, Jake Hess, or the rest of the Statesmen move on in the program. The audience demanded that they just keep singing "Happy Rhythm." As the quartet sang it again and again, more folks stood on chairs, jumped in the aisles, and eventually sang right along with them. The Statesmen had never seen anything like it. They had come to Georgia for a gospel concert, and a dance had broken out.

When they called Lister and told him how the song had been received, he wasn't surprised. He had come to realize that "Happy Rhythm" spoke to the real happiness that could be found through salvation and a life spent living in the Spirit. Even Lister wanted to jump and shout every time he sang it.

"'Happy Rhythm' was really a song that expressed the joy of being a Christian," Lister explained. "People who know God express their joy in a lot of different ways; I belong to a church that could sing happy songs. On a Sunday morning in my church 'Happy Rhythm' would not seem out of place."

The Statesmen released "Happy Rhythm" as a single, and the song stormed the gospel music world of the early fifties. In time they noticed that more and more teenagers were showing up to catch their performances. These young people might not have been too impressed with some of the old standards, but when the Big Chief led off with "Happy Rhythm," the kids got into it. They seemed to think this was a gospel song that came from their musical culture. In the word of the day, they "grooved" with it.

Considered in the context of where gospel music has gone today, "Happy Rhythm" hardly rates as a novel concept. But when Lister wrote it and the Statesmen made it their own, this "rockin'" number was so far ahead of its time that it stood apart from every gospel song that had come before it. Inspired in lyrics, emotions, and words, this enthusiastic mix of black and white influences not only made Christians jump for joy but also forecast the sounds that would storm the radio and concert halls in secular music for years to come.

When Mosie Lister was moved to write that song in 1953, he expressed his own emotions about faith. "Happy Rhythm" forced folks to feel happy about being saved and walking the Christian walk. It was a song that pointed out that it was all right to have fun and be a Christian. It was a message that the young, who were often called square if they got involved in church, needed to hear.

In the early seventies gospel musicians recognized that by using the contemporary sounds of music, vast numbers of young people could be drawn to the Lord. This was something Lister and the Statesmen had discovered that night in 1953. Their "Happy Rhythm" was the first contemporary Christian hit.

Heaven Came Down

In World War II twenty-three-year-old John Peterson was flying bombers over the Himalayan Mountains. He often encountered Japanese enemy pilots whose fighting passion was unlike anything he had ever seen before, and for the young Kansas Army Air Corps pilot, life was now lived moment to moment. Before each flight Peterson prayed hard for the miracle that would bring him back safely over the hell on earth that was the "China Hump." Each day, in spite of the odds, his prayers were answered.

Saved by Christ at the age of eleven and saved from death in the flames of battle as a young man, this devout Christian believed God's hand had been on him each step of his life. He knew it was the Lord who had seen him through the bitter and the sweet. He lived his faith so strongly that all those around him recognized it in his every action. So it came as no surprise when after his wartime duty was completed, he returned to the United States and enrolled in the Moody Bible Institute. After graduating from Moody he moved on to the American Conservatory of Music and then to a post as the editor of Singspiration. Peterson had fully given his life to the business of spreading the gospel through music.

Singspiration's offices were located in Montrose, Pennsylvania. In part because of the publisher's presence, each year the city hosted the Montrose Bible Conference. A regular at the meetings in 1961, Peterson, who had been composing cantatas and choral arrangements for more than a decade, was inspired to create a gospel music classic.

He had been leading the music during a worship session when an elderly gentleman stood up and asked to address the crowd. As he began to give his testimony, the audience grew hushed. The speaker's obvious sincerity and simple, humble tone moved Peterson to lean forward and listen very closely. As he looked into the man's eyes, Peterson deeply felt his emotional words and could sense the love God had brought into his life.

When the man used the phrase "it seemed like heaven came down and glory filled my soul," Peterson immediately grabbed a scrap piece of paper and jotted the line down. He then quickly looked back up so he could listen to the remainder of the man's short testimony. Although many seemed to be touched by what the old man had shared, no one but Peterson had been moved to record any of those brief moments. And as beautiful as was the story and as haunting as was the image, it is doubtful that even he would have remembered any of the man's words if he hadn't written them down.

Caught up in duties at the conference, it was a few days before John had a chance to glance back at the words he had written: "heaven came down and glory filled my soul." When he did, the old man's entire testimony rushed back and filled the music man's mind, heart, and soul.

Like many country music songwriters, John Peterson believed most great songs were born from a single line or a simple experience. A word or phrase, spoken at the right moment, was like a seed. When planted as an idea and given the proper attention and care, this seed would grow into a plant bearing much fruit. John had seen this happen time and time again in his work, such as in another song he had written: "No One Understands Like Jesus." Now, with the image of a silver-haired believer etched deeply in Peterson's mind, a single line would again inspire an entire song.

"Heaven Came Down" took very little time to write. Using the man's testimony as the framework and the copied line as the central theme, Peterson in his imagination became the old man who had stood and addressed the crowd. While sitting at his desk, he allowed himself to imagine the feelings of rapture of coming to know Christ in such a powerful manner. Soon the emotions that had poured out at the service were alive in Peterson's heart too. The most dramatic moment of the old man's life was as real to him as flying planes had been during World War II.

Matching music to his verses, Peterson published "Heaven Came Down" in his own songbooks just months after he had written it. It quickly became a choral favorite and found its way into scores of hymnals. Much more than Peterson's other works, "Heaven Came Down" was taken in a very personal way into the hearts of thousands of believers. Largely because of the relationship between the song and individuals, this singing testimony was quickly thought of as a gospel classic in the vein of Brumley, Stanphill, and Dorsey.

"Heaven Came Down" is a song about hope, joy, compassion, and faith. It is a powerful work that is simply phrased. It is a personal testimony that transcends individuals, denominations, and experiences. It is the complete salvation experience taken from the soul of a single believer and transformed into a work that touches all believers.

When John Peterson was a small child, his grandfather told him that someday he would write words that would change the world. In the dark days of World War II, when it seemed unlikely that John would even survive long enough to write another letter home, this prediction hardly seemed possible.

Yet just as he believed that God brought him through the perils of fighting and safely home, he also believed that God placed an old man with a wonderful story in a service where he was directing the music. Although it was not originally his own testimony, Peterson's faith and life were never more clearly presented than in "Heaven Came Down."

He Keeps Me Singing

*I*n 1901 Luther Bridgers accepted the call to full-time Christian work during a service in his North Carolina church. The seventeen-year-old knew the decision to become a minister ended any dreams of wealth or fame. He realized his life would be spent moving from town to town, constantly making new friends, endlessly facing new challenges, and being expected to make the right decisions in even the toughest situations. As those around him would say time and time again, "Luther, now you have to walk a higher road." "You have to set an example for others; you cannot slip or backslide." "You shouldn't show or admit doubt; you must be strong no matter what kind of situations confront you." As time would prove, the young man took these words to heart.

Bridgers attended Assembly College in Wilmore, Kentucky, studied his Bible, and developed not only his skill in the pulpit but also his ability to touch hearts in one-on-one conversations. Outgoing, happy, and filled with an enthusiasm that outweighed his own natural fears, he accepted his first pastorate in a tiny Methodist Church with an energy and devotion to duty that brought immediate trust.

The preacher quickly won over not only his congregation but also a pretty young woman. He and this young woman were married and began a family. Although they often were forced to live on little money and few niceties, the Bridgers made up for what they didn't have with love. Devoted to each other and to Christ, the family was a role model for all the young married couples in the area. The laughter that came from their home proved the joy they knew in their daily lives. If God had ever joined two people together for a lifetime of fellowship and service, it seemed it was these two.

In 1910 Luther regretfully said good-bye to his wife and toddlers in order to take a short trip. Although he hated to leave his family to preach at a revival in another town, he knew the journey and the week in a strange town would be too hard on them. He was greatly relieved when his father-in-law offered his home to the family. With peace in his heart, Luther left his Kentucky home confident that if any emergency should arise, a man he deeply trusted would be there to guide his wife and three children through it. With his concerns about his family taken care of, he devoted his energy and study to his task.

Although the revival was going well, those who had come to know Bridgers during his visit realized he looked forward to wrapping up the week of services and returning home. Over meals and in his messages he was constantly telling stories about his wife and children. Even those he had just met were sure of the joy he felt in being a husband and a father.

One cool night, as Luther prayed for the few who had walked down the aisle and accepted the will of the Lord in their lives, disaster struck in Harroldsburg, Kentucky. At the very time Luther's words were bringing peace to those who heard his sermon, a fire broke out, trapping his wife and three children in a burning house. The heat of the inferno was too great and the flames too all-consuming for anyone to respond to their cries for help. With friends and family looking on, the four members of the Bridgers family died horrible deaths.

Hearing that his family had perished, Luther was overcome with grief. After he returned home and as he looked at the four caskets and met with those who had witnessed the tragedy, he seemed to be in shock. Some of those around him expected him to crack under the pressure. Many of the unsaved in the community were watching for him to curse the God who had snatched the innocent loved ones from his life. Yet in the face of such unimaginable pain, Bridgers went forward, not cursing, not blaming, not asking why. His faith seemingly unshaken, he comforted others whose doubts had been stirred by the fiery, tragic deaths.

In an attempt to explain to those around him the faith he still had in his heart, Luther set his emotions to words and music. In tear-filled hours he took up a pen and wrote what was on his heart and in his mind. Even while acknowledging his own pain, he spelled out his unwavering trust.

"He Keeps Me Singing" was published in *The Revival* songbook by Charlie D. Tillman within months of the fire that claimed the lives of the four people Bridgers held most dear. Within a year it had become one of the most popular new gospel songs in the nation. Used at singing schools and conventions, arranged for quartet and choral presentations, the song born from a deadly fire has brought deep joy to millions of hearts for almost nine decades. "He Keeps Me Singing" is still consistently picked as one of America's ten favorite gospel songs.

Four years after losing his family, Luther remarried and became a full-time evangelist. During World War I he did mission work in Europe and Russia. As both evangelist and pastor he served the Lord each day of his life until his death in 1948. Although he never understood why he had so tragically lost his family, he never questioned it either. He had accepted a call to lead by example, and even in the face of the greatest loss a man can feel, he did so. The Lord gave him the faith to anchor him and bring him needed strength. Thus, even in his grief, Luther Bridgers was able to explain his faith in a song. Little did he guess that so many people would be greatly inspired and know such joy, thanks to his song "He Keeps Me Singing."

He Knows Just What I Need

To many it may seem that Mosie Lister was born to write music. His music is that special. What may surprise many is that Lister himself believes that God put music in him at birth. Writing music was a path he felt destined to follow.

"I grew up in family gospel," the songwriter recalled. "I sang as a teen in a family group. You have to understand that my father and mother loved gospel music very much. We sang all the time. And when I wasn't singing with them, I sang at church. Yet even at the age of five, before I had ever sung in public, before I could even read the music in a songbook, I wanted to be able to write music. It may be hard to believe, but even at that young age I knew that writing music was what I wanted to do when I grew up."

Lister began writing words and trying to come up with new melodies at about the same time he learned to read. He seemed driven by this yearning to create. While others were playing baseball, he studied harmony and theory at a singing school. While others listened to sporting events on the radio, he tuned in to symphonies. While other kids read comic books, he searched for any book on music that he could find, then read each of them, not once, but many times.

"I guess I almost memorized all the music books I read," he explained. "At night, when I was falling asleep, I would think of what I had read and heard. I recall when I was a young teenager being able to hear in my head choirs and big bands of trumpets, violins, and brass. I would often lie awake at night imagining thousands of voices singing wonderful music."

After briefly singing with a quartet in the early forties, the Georgia farm boy entered the Navy. When World War II ended and he returned from service, he wasted no time putting together the Sunny South Quartet. Their home base was Tampa, Florida. He stayed with the group until he ran into an old friend.

"Although he was no relation to me," Lister explained, "I knew and admired Hovie Lister a great deal. At that time he was playing piano for the Rangers Quartet. When I decided to return to my home state and start a new quartet—Statesmen—in Atlanta, Hovie worked with me. We got Big Chief Weathington to sing bass, I sang lead, and that was the foundation of the group. After a while, when I got tired of the traveling, Jake Hess took my place. I still worked with the Statesmen, only I cut back my contributions to arranging and song writing."

Although he was having to supplement his income as a piano tuner, Lister still found time to write a great amount of original material. It seemed to flow out of him like water.

"I believe that the music had always been inside me," Lister explained. "God had put it there and when I started to write, it just came out. What I had learned in my studies and through my experiences just helped me better understand what God had placed in my heart."

By 1955 Lister had begun to establish himself as one of the premier songwriters in southern gospel music. Yet while enthusiastically accepted in this market, his work had a totally different feel from that of most other writers in the genre. His songs were more contemporary and seemingly much more intimate.

"I wrote songs out of my own personal experiences and my own desire to know and serve the Lord better and to experience Him more fully," Lister pointed out. "When I wrote a song, I wanted to say things I felt strongly about. I wanted people to know I lived by the words I had written. I didn't just say that I could always depend on God, I believed it. So when I began to compose 'He Knows Just What I Need,' it was more like my testimony put to music than just a theme I wrote about."

Of all the wonderful songs he has written, Lister is probably the most passionate about this song. Carefully crafted, each phrase a study in individual faith, this song represents the writer's life. It is his faith put into words and music.

"I really believe God does know when we are lonely and have heartaches," Lister said. "More important, when we are down, He cares. I wanted everyone who heard this song to know the Lord was always there for them."

Because of the importance placed on the message of "He Knows Just What I Need," Lister worked with the lyrics far longer than he did with many of his other compositions. He didn't want to put any stumbling blocks in the words. He didn't want to leave something that might be misinterpreted by a lost person searching for answers. This led to his even taking the verses to theologians to have them evaluate the song's message, truth, and impact.

"Something not very many people know," the writer recalled about his most intimate work, "is that after a while I went back and changed one line. In my mind 'He understands because He cares' didn't sound right. I was at a loss to know how to make the line right, so I took the song to a Bible scholar. He looked at it and told me, 'God understands because He is God.' With that in mind, I reworked the line to read, 'He understands and always cares.' When I sang it again, I realized this was a lot closer to my own understanding of faith.

"When I finished writing and rewriting 'He Knows Just What I Need,' I took it to the Statesmen. They liked up-tempo songs, so I thought they would sing it that way. I was surprised when I first heard them do it. They sang it very slowly. Of course I quickly realized the slow tempo gave more depth to the words. When Elvis cut it a few years later, he did it just as the Statesmen had."

"I think that Mosie Lister is one of the greatest songwriters in any field to ever pick up a pen," proclaimed Cathedral bass legend George Younce. "Yet as great a songwriter as he is, he is even a better person. He writes what he lives, so both his songs and his life inspire everyone who meets him."

"He Knows Just What I Need" represents Lister better than any other song he ever wrote. It is his testimony. Yet in truth, there is a part of his Christian walk in every one of his songs. He believes he was put here by God to write gospel music. "It thrills me that some of things I have written have strengthened the faith of other people," Lister says humbly. "That is the reason I write songs."

As is obvious in the message proclaimed in each of his works, he knows just what we need. He gives it to us in everything he writes.

He Looked Beyond My Fault and Saw My Need

When Dottie was just a small child, she began to write lyrics and simple melodies effortlessly. By the time she was ten she had taught herself to play an older brother's guitar and was honing a talent that seemed to be inborn. By the age of twelve she had accepted the Lord as her Savior and given her life completely to writing Christian songs.

While her mother encouraged her to grow as a writer and as a Christian, her father demanded that she give up both her music and her "obsession" with her faith. Although she tried to be respectful of his opinion, she was resolute in her own calling. She continued to write, perform, and share her message of hope not only with those in her church but also with her teenage friends. At sixteen she married one of those friends, Buck Rambo, and together the couple began to use Dottie's writing and singing talents to carve out a career in gospel music.

The Rambos first gained national exposure with a southern gospel group, the Dixie Echoes. The heart of the group and the star of every performance was the small, pretty Dottie. Her sincerity was unquestionable, her devotion to serving Jesus seemed completely natural, and her remarkable self-penned songs sung with her sweet, lilting voice seemed to go straight to each listener's heart. It was a combination that would make the Dixie Echoes one of southern gospel music's most beloved groups.

Although Dottie has composed more than 2,500 songs, a few stand out not only above her other efforts but also above those of almost every other inspirational songwriter. This tiny woman's writing talent places her on a par with Mosie Lister, Thomas A. Dorsey, Bill Gaither, Albert E. Brumley, and E.M. Bartlett. And like the works of these giants, Dottie's efforts were almost always inspired by events taken from her own life.

One of her most remarkable songs, "He Looked Beyond My Fault and Saw My Need," was written as a message to her brother. Just a few years older than Dottie, Eddy had been her best friend through much of their youth. Yet while Dottie had embraced Christ and a life of Christian service, Eddy had drifted into a life of drinking, lying, cheating, and crime. There were many times Dottie would go to bed wondering where Eddy was, what he was doing, and if he was still alive. No matter what his physical and spiritual state, she always thankfully prayed when she heard that he was all right.

Most people figured Eddy would eventually learn his lesson and straighten up. Yet when he didn't, the courts finally grew tired of giving him second chances. Dottie prayed that behind prison walls Eddy would wake up. Yet in spite of her own witness and in spite of the efforts of other family members and friends who tried to lead Eddy to Christ, he simply refused to take the Word or the message seriously. He was proud of his sister; he was happy to tell people she was an award-winning recording artist and a songwriter. He just wasn't going to buy into what her songs were selling.

When Eddy was released from prison and got back on the streets, there were many nights he came to hear his sister sing. Dottie could tell that he enjoyed her work, but she couldn't help but notice that just before she gave an invitation to accept the Lord, her brother would always slip out the back door. No matter the ultimate cost, no matter his own fear of death, he was not willing to change his own life or accept Jesus into his heart. He figured he had plenty of time to come to that decision, but he soon discovered that even his days were numbered.

When Dottie found out that Eddy had cancer, it scared her and nearly broke her heart. She knew that he was an unrepentant sinner, and she knew that if he didn't turn and repent he would spend eternity in hell.

For many weeks she visited Eddy in his hospital room. During this time his condition grew worse and his attitude about his own fate became more resolved. When they spoke of spiritual matters, the young man told his sister he didn't deserve to go to heaven. He thought he had done nothing to earn that reward. Although it was not too late for the thief crucified with Jesus, Eddy seemed to think it was too late for him.

Knowing her brother had just weeks to live, Dottie began to pray for him at every opportunity. Eddy's failure to accept Christ and his viewpoint that he was not worthy of salvation haunted her. Finally she was driven to express her own pain and heartache the way she always did—she was driven to write. As she took a pen in hand, the words she wanted to share with her brother flowed out as easily as if she had known them all her life.

Dottie didn't write original music to go with her very short, simple verses. She set the new lyrics to a very sad old English folk song, "Danny Boy." Not only did the meter fit this well-known tune, but the theme of the original song, that of a young soldier dying before he had had much of a chance to live, seemed to mesh with her brother's situation as well. Taking only the time to learn the words well enough to sing them from memory, Dottie rushed back to the hospital to share them with Eddy.

As he had at many of her concerts and services, Eddy listened intently to his sister as she sang. Yet this time, phrases like "it was grace that bought my liberty," and "He looked beyond my fault and saw my need," did more than resonate in his head, they touched his heart. Before she left, he asked Dottie to write down the song's lyrics. As she left his room, he intently studied those words.

A few weeks later Eddy died. Cancer had so consumed his body that he weighed little more than a six-year-old child. Yet during those final, tough weeks, Eddy was buoyant, his spirit was soaring, he was as happy as he had ever been. Thanks in large part to her witness and her song, Dottie Rambo's brother had come to know the Lord as his Savior.

Dottie cannot sing "He Looked Beyond My Fault and Saw My Need" without thinking of Eddy. When she sings, she doesn't remember the wild child or the young man wandering on a path of sin. Rather, she thinks of the happy soul who found that Christ can forgive anyone of any transgression. Thus the words to "He Looked Beyond My Fault and Saw My Need" come alive in a special way each night, each concert, each time Dottie lends her voice to them. If you listen, you will be able to hear the message that saved the soul of dying man.

He Touched Me

$\mathcal{B}$ill Gaither was working as a high school teacher and part-time church music director when he was invited to play the piano at a revival meeting in Huntington, Indiana. It was a rare night that he could have spent with his wife and children. Others could have done the job. Certainly no one would have blamed the busy Gaither for begging off and watching television or working on new arrangements for his trio. Yet it wouldn't have been like him to ignore a call to share his talents in a Christian forum; so his wife and two daughters knew that he would have to leave them to honor this request. As it turned out, if he hadn't gone that night he might have never become the focal point of gospel music in the seventies and eighties, and the song that most feel is his best might have never been written.

The speaker that evening was Dr. Dale Oldham. Dale's son Doug provided the special music. It was a very successful service, with many people making decisions to follow Jesus. Even though he missed his family, Bill knew it was a night well spent.

As he rode back to his Anderson home with the Oldhams, he remarked about how he had been touched by the Spirit during the service. Dale added that he saw many other people who had been touched by the Spirit too. All three men came to the conclusion it had been one of those rare evenings when everyone had felt the presence of the Holy Spirit. Like those who had come to hear their messages, they themselves had been deeply blessed.

It was very early in the morning when Dale dropped Bill off at his home, but the preacher didn't let him go inside until he told him, "You should write a song that says, 'He touched me; oh, He touched me.'" After Bill had gone to bed those words continued to turn over in his mind until they finally forced him out of bed and to the piano. That was where his wife found him early that Sunday morning.

Bill had noted that a great many people who had come to the revival meeting appeared to be carrying a very heavy load of guilt and pain. There was no energy in their step and no sparkle in their eyes. Yet as they were touched by the music and the message, as they became caught up in the thoughts of a living, caring, loving God, their burdens seemed to be lifted. Many who had come to the service depressed and downcast left wearing the glow of happiness and joy.

Using these images coupled with the line Dale Oldham had suggested, Bill crafted a very simple set of verses attached to an elementary melody. Maybe because everything was so direct and uncluttered the message shone through as bright as a summer sun. Even as he sang it through the first time, he must have realized this was a song almost anyone could sing.

Bill's wife, Gloria, was caught up in the song's passion. She could sense real emotion in every line. Even though she had not attended the revival, the song made her feel as revived as if she had been on the front pew. As a matter of fact, when Bill played it all for her, she had only one suggestion. She wanted him to replace a line she thought was too weak. Bill listened, made a mental note, and considered her observation.

"Fortunately," Gloria admits, "Bill kept the line as it was. He felt that the phrase simply and completely stated what he had seen on the faces at the service."

Within a week Doug Oldham was performing the song at revival meetings and concerts. He thought it was his story. This sense of ownership seemed strange because Bill considered it his own testimony. However, Bill soon discovered that the song seemed to describe every believer's view of Christ, and for him it would become much more.

Doug was the first to record "He Touched Me," but not the last. Several more southern gospel artists, including the Imperials, immediately cut it. The quartet had become a favorite of high school and college students and was as hot as any other southern gospel group in the nation. When the Imperials weren't singing in churches and on campuses, they were touring with Elvis Presley's road show.

It was no secret that the rock idol had always loved gospel music. Although the crowds who flocked to the national quartet convention didn't know it, Elvis was a regular back stage at most of the shows. On those occasions he often invited scores of top acts to his house for all-night gospel singings. He also never traveled without a gospel group in tow.

When Elvis heard the Imperials, he made arrangements to take them on the road as his backup group. Not only did he and the quartet use gospel music to warm up before the show but also during each of his concerts Presley stepped away from center stage and asked the Imperials to perform a gospel number on their own. One night they premiered their version of "He Touched Me" for the rocker's fans. Elvis was so overcome by the power of the song that he featured it every night as long as the Imperials traveled with him.

In 1969 Elvis cut "He Touched Me" and won a Grammy for his recording. Thanks in large part to the exposure given it by Elvis, scores of others cut the song too. It wasn't surprising that top voices in southern and black gospel music put it on their albums, as most Christian artists tried to place their spin on the hottest new compositions. Yet what wasn't expected was that Kate Smith, Jimmy Durante, and dozens of other secular acts recorded it too. It quickly became the biggest Christian hit in more than a decade and perhaps the most recorded true southern gospel song ever.

"He Touched Me" launched Bill Gaither's career. After more than a decade of hard work, he was an overnight success. Bill won the Gospel Music Association's Songwriter of the Year Dove award every year for more than a decade. It seemed that everyone wanted to cut anything Gaither wrote.

Gospel music is music that brings the Holy Spirit into the heart. It is music that touches and heals. It brings joy and comfort. It lifts souls toward heaven and fuels a passion for doing the Lord's work. It inspires more than it entertains. Most of all, gospel music creates an atmosphere that allows Jesus Christ to come into lives. "He Touched Me" is a special song that fully defines what every gospel song tries to be.

Bill Gaither was overwhelmed by the success and power of "He Touched Me." He had prayed for a vehicle that would allow him to give his life full time to God's work. He had long hoped for a chance to spend every spare hour in the creation of Christian music. Yet he had never expected one song to make it all possible.

Gaither once told writer Chet Hagan, "A song like that is just born of the mystical presence of Christ—a change in your life. There's still nothing as touching or as moving as the first-person testimony of someone coming forward and saying, 'I had no hope. I was down. Then the hand of Jesus touched me.'"

In trying to define the testimonies of a few who had made decisions at a revival, Gaither wrote down everyone's testimony. Although it appeals to the masses, "He Touched Me" is really a very personal song that speaks to individuals. That is why it not only made Bill Gaither a shining star in the world of Christian music but also has come to define what gospel music really is.

His Eye Is on the Sparrow

In 1904 Civilla Martin, the wife of a well-known evangelist, was involved in conducting revival services in Elmira, New York. Through her work she heard of an older couple who had once been beacons in the church but in recent times had been felled by illness and injury. The world of the homebound, usually bedridden couple had shrunk from an activity-filled existence in church and community to a house of two or three rooms.

Civilla, who traveled extensively and who relished the freedom of waking each week in a new location, couldn't begin to imagine how this once-active couple could face each day. As they were shut in, devoid of the pleasures of life, their bodies racked by pain, she pictured them bitter and withdrawn. Yet the more she heard about what they had accomplished in the past and how much they had meant to the city and the church congregation, the more she felt called to at least pay them a visit. Still, she avoided visiting them until she discovered that they had been inquiring about the success of the revival. Hearing that they had been praying for the Martins' work, Civilla, no matter how busy, tired, and exhausted she was, seemed to have no choice but to go to their home and meet them.

She had expected to enter a dark, foreboding house, reeking of death and decay; instead, she was warmly welcomed into a home filled with life and joy. From the cheery living room she was led to a small bedroom, the windows and drapes open wide to let in rays of sunshine and the smell of fresh flowers. Lying in bed, her body withered and drawn, her skin pale, was a woman gamely fighting a ravaging disease. When she observed Civilla at her door, rather than moan or frown, she laughed as a smile spread across her face. To Civilla's surprise, as she looked into the bedridden woman's eyes she didn't see death, she saw life.

Sitting beside the bed, Civilla was quickly taken in by this woman who seemed to ignore her own pain, suffering, and heartache while asking about others who were far less sick than she. Although she was weak in body, the woman's spirit was as strong as any Civilla had ever seen. Soon the two woman were joined by the man of the house. His body, too, was spent, but like his wife, he was cheerful, unselfish, and content with the lot he had been given.

"How can you be so joyful?" Civilla finally asked. "What can drive your spirits in the midst of such pain and suffering?"

A happy smile crossed the woman's face, and with a trembling hand she pointed to the window. Civilla glanced out into the yard and saw nothing but trees, grass, and a few flowers. With a puzzled look on her face, she turned back to the woman.

"It's the sparrows, child," the woman replied. "If His eye is on the sparrows, then I know He watches me too."

Nodding, her husband smiled and looked back at the birds playing in the tree. There was a joy that exuded from both of them as the small birds fluttered about.

Civilla left uplifted in both spirit and body. No longer drained by a week of work, no longer feeling the aches and pains caused by stress, she had been set free as never before. She almost felt as if she could fly. She had come to Elmira to lead a revival, but she was the one who had been revived.

After reviewing the texts that she found in Luke 12:6 and Matthew 10:29, Civilla picked up a pen and jotted down the line, "His eye in on the sparrow and I know He watches me." As she thought of the sickly couple, considering their plight and their happiness, the words that followed came easily.

Civilla Martin mailed her poem to composer Charles H. Gabriel. Setting the words to music, Gabriel then sent the song to Charles M. Alexander. Alexander showed it to London evangelist R.A. Torrey. Torrey was excited about the lyrics and the music. He built a sermon around the song and asked that it be sung during services at the Royal Albert Hall. Never before had a gospel song premiered in such a prestigious setting.

Because of the unique tune and cadence that Gabriel had developed for the song, "His Eye Is on the Sparrow" never became a religious standard. While the song's message is universal, it is not suited for congregational singing nor does it fit well into choral work. It was so personally written that it is usually deemed fit only for solo work. Thus "His Eye Is on the Sparrow" did not enjoy the wide-spread popularity of most hymns of the period. Even Civilla Martin's own "God Will Take Care of You" quickly eclipsed this inspired song.

More than four decades after Martin had written it, another woman emerged who seemed created just to sing this song. Ethel Waters had been born in 1900 in Chester, Pennsylvania. An actress, cabaret performer, and blues singer, she had a network radio show in the thirties and appeared in Hollywood films during the forties. Although she was a vital facet of a world that often seemed adrift in sin, Waters not only kept her priorities in order, but she also constantly spoke out about her faith. Using her vocal talents, she sang gospel songs in night clubs and churches, reaching both the lost and the saved with the Good News.

A young evangelist named Billy Graham heard Ethel sing "His Eye Is on the Sparrow" and was overcome with emotion. He convinced her to sing the song at his crusades. Thanks in large part to her exposure on the Graham crusades, Waters jumped to the forefront in the gospel music world. Along with Tennessee Ernie Ford and Mahalia Jackson, she represented to many the emotions and feelings of saved souls. Her signature song, "His Eye Is on the Sparrow," constantly brought hope to millions who had once felt insignificant, forgotten, and lost.

In 1971 a frail and ill Ethel Waters performed at the Nixon White House. The president had only one request of the seventy-one-year-old African-American vocalist. "Please sing 'His Eye Is on the Sparrow,'" he asked. As always, her rendition brought tears of joy from those who had gathered to hear her.

Just as Civilla Martin could not question the sincerity of the old couple who had first inspired her, so no one at the White House that day could question the sincerity and faith of Ms. Waters. She was truly singing because she was happy and free. Most importantly, thanks to a song about a tiny bird, everyone could feel her joy and fly!

His Hand in Mine

There are many who believe that if a song doesn't come together quickly, it will never come together at all. Yet for some writers, creation is an ongoing experience that may last days, months, and years. Sometimes the marriage of words and melody is bridged by a wealth of experience and a great deal of prayer. Even masters such as Mosie Lister often have to live with a work in progress for a long time before they receive the final inspiration that brings everything together.

"In the early fifties I was working for a Georgia piano store," Lister recalled. "I hadn't yet made a step of faith and given my life completely to writing. As a part of my job with the store I made calls on customers, worked on their pianos in their homes, and when I had gotten the instrument tuned or fixed, I'd sit in front of the keyboard and play something to get a feel for how it sounded. Although I don't know why, on a day when I was playing at this one home, I lost myself in the keyboard. I just kept playing a melody that was new to me. I had never heard it, and I had no idea for words to go with that melody. I just knew I liked it, and I kept playing it over and over again."

For about a year Lister played the unknown song everywhere he worked on pianos. Day after day, week after week he would lose himself in that melody. At each piano he tested and in each home he visited, he played that same song as a final test of his work. Finally, at one home a woman asked him what the song's name was. It was a question he couldn't answer.

"I told her it was just something I had been playing for a while," Lister explained. "It's just an unfinished work."

The answer seemed to disappoint the woman. She had wanted to hear the message behind the beautiful melody. Her desires were not unlike his own. Her questions also triggered in him a sudden need to finish his work.

The house where he had been working was more than sixty miles from his home in Atlanta. On the long drive down the two-lane blacktop back to the city, Lister began to play the tune over and over again in his mind. As the miles passed, frustration brought on by a lack of closure began to weigh on him.

"My pastor had once told me," Lister recalled, "if you want to talk to God, just pretend He is a close friend or a family member. When you do that you can easily tell God exactly what you feel. That is what I did that day. Just talked to the Lord as if He were sitting in the car with me."

As Lister began to pray, he was overcome with emotion. Afraid to continue his journey with so many things other than driving flooding his mind, he pulled over to the side of the road. After safely getting his car out of traffic, he bowed his head and began to pour out his troubles to God.

"I remember feeling an urge to finish the song I had been playing," Lister explained, "and that is what I needed to talk about. So I prayed, 'Lord, you understand me, I believe this song is something you want me to write. I need some help writing the words. Please reach out to me.'"

After he finished his prayer, Lister maneuvered back into traffic and headed home. As soon as he walked into his house, he picked up a pen and paper and quickly jotted down the words that meshed with his melody.

"I still don't know the process," he admitted. "I don't know how the words came to me. As I wrote them I just knew that

God was real and He was answering my prayer. I called my wife into the room and told her I wanted to sing my new song for her. She thought it was beautiful."

Over the course of the next few days, Lister sang it many times and made a few changes. Each time a phrase was cleaned up, he felt God was directing him each step of the way. Finally, when he had worked the phrase "His hand in mine" into a bridge, he was ready to share his creation with someone in the music business.

"I showed it to the Statesmen in 1953," Lister remembered, "but they passed on it. They wanted something more up-tempo. While they liked 'His Hand in Mine,' they didn't want a ballad. The Crusaders were the first to record it. Then the Blackwood Brothers picked it up a year later. Eventually the Statesmen recorded it too."

By the mid-fifties almost every southern gospel group was singing "His Hand in Mine." The song not only paved the way for Lister to leave his day job and give himself completely to writing sacred music, it also brought him a degree of financial security. Thanks to the Blackwoods' and Statesmen's cut of "His Hand in Mine," Elvis Presley heard the song and chose it as the title track for his first gospel album. Sales of Presley's "His Hand in Mine" were so strong that Lister was getting air play and marking up sales not only across the United States but also in more than two dozen foreign countries.

Although Mosie Lister cannot put a finger on how he wrote the melody or where he found the inspiration to compose the words to his best-known gospel music classic, he does know that a short prayer changed his life forever. By pulling off to the side of a road and giving his heart and problems to God, he not only found answers to one simple prayer, he was also given a road to his dreams.

How Great Thou Art

There can be little doubt that "Amazing Grace" and "How Great Thou Art" are the two most popular Christian songs in the world. Although these two gospel standards have come to be strongly identified with America and cherished as products of the Christian movements of this nation, both of them were inspired and composed by events half a world away from the United States.

When George Beverly Shea sang "How Great Thou Art" at a Billy Graham Crusade in Toronto in 1955, many thought a newly written gospel song was being premiered. As Shea sang "How Great Thou Art" night after night in cities all around the world, and as he, Tennessee Ernie Ford, and countless others rushed into the recording studios to cut their versions of this emerging classic, it became an overnight sensation at churches, conventions, and concerts and on the radio. Never before had a religious song become so universally recognized so quickly. Although Stuart K. Hine's name is listed as the song's writer, in reality it was a young Swedish preacher, Carl Boberg, who initially composed the first few stanzas. On a summer day in the early 1880s, Boberg was caught in a raging thunderstorm. As he sought shelter, he watched in awe the flashes of blinding lightning, the mighty winds, and the torrent of water that fell from the skies. He wondered how he or any other living thing could survive such an onslaught. Yet as quickly as the storm had struck, it disappeared, leaving a damp but beautiful world in its wake.

As amazed as he was by the storm's sudden power and intensity, the pastor was equally struck by the brilliant sunshine and singing birds that came immediately at the storm's end. With the fragrance of life all around him and a rainbow seemingly directing his way home, Boberg felt an incredible sense of renewal. With the thoughts of these events fresh in his mind, he wrote nine stanzas of poetry describing what he had been privileged to witness. He shared these words with his congregation in the form of a song set to an old folk melody. By 1886, *"O Store Gud"* was not only a favorite of Pastor Boberg's congregation, but it had also been published and was being used in worship services throughout Sweden.

By 1907 Boberg's original lyrics had been translated into German. Soon after World War I, *"O Store Gud"* found its way into Russian hymnals too. In 1927, while working as a missionary in the Ukraine, Englishman Stuart K. Hine happened upon the Russian version of the song during his work in the region's churches. Several years later he translated the first stanza into English. As he traveled throughout Europe, he translated Boberg's next two stanzas, rewriting them and adding as much of his own inspiration as he borrowed from the original author's text. Although he used the song from time to time in his missionary work, he made no attempt to have "How Great Thou Art" published.

When World War II broke out, Hine returned home. For the next ten years he stayed in England, occasionally pulling out his version of the song to share with others.

In 1948 he visited a refugee camp in Sussex, England. There, among a group of hundreds of Russians who were fleeing communism, Hine witnessed two Christian men sharing with others the power of salvation. Moved by the refugees' Christian commitment and their message, he added a final stanza to "How Great Thou Art" that spelled out the joy these men foresaw in the second coming of Christ.

Hine sought out and found a small publisher who printed the song in leaflet form. One of these manuscripts was handed to Billy Graham's soloist George Beverly Shea at the end of a service. Deeply moved by both the song's message and music, Shea brought "How Great Thou Art" to Dr. Graham. The two decided it would work perfectly with the text of the evangelist's next message. Little did either realize that on that night the sermon's words would pale against the message of "How Great Thou Art."

The power and reach of Billy Graham's crusades allowed Carl Boberg's and Stuart Hine's inspirational words and music to quickly circle the globe. Within just a few years "How Great Thou Art" had become as well known and easily recognized as "Jesus Loves Me." It was used by church choirs, quartets, trios, duos, and solo artists. It was sung at the Met, Buckingham Palace, the Hollywood Bowl, and the *Grand Ole Opry*, in churches around the world, and on the mission fields of the Third World. Translated into scores of languages and dialects, the song has become one of the most effective tools of evangelism ever created.

Carl Boberg had once been so awed by a summer thunderstorm that he recorded his emotions so his parishioners could feel the divine power he had witnessed firsthand. If he had been able to see the truly divine nature of his efforts, then he might have been completely awed by the message for which he lived. "How Great Thou Art" is not only a song that beautifully describes the nature of the Lord but also a testament to how much one man's faith in God can mean to others.

I'd Rather Have Jesus

George Beverly Shea is probably the best-known and most loved gospel music singer in the world. In gospel music he is an icon, a legend, and a role model. With his deep, rich voice and his sincere walk with the Lord, to countless Christians he represents gospel music in its most meaningful form. His many years with the Billy Graham Crusades took him to every corner of the globe, exposed his music and his faith to tens of millions of people, and established the songs he sang as the most familiar inspirational pieces in history. Yet he wasn't always only a gospel singer; it had taken some time for him to find his life's calling.

"We—that is, my parents and I—moved from Canada to New York when I was in my early twenties," Shea explained. "I worked as a clerk in the Mutual Life Insurance Building on Wall Street. I knew the Lord as my Savior but didn't know where He was going to lead me."

At this time radio had exploded onto the American scene, and New York was home to thousands of men and women trying to find fame and fortune in show business. Many were doing almost anything to get an opportunity to be on radio. The times were electric, and though Shea didn't want to juggle or spin yarns, he did find the lure of the airwaves very tempting.

"I was enjoying those early days of radio," Shea remembered. "Fred Allen, the comedian, was hosting an amateur hour, and I got on the show. I won second prize. A yodeler beat me."

Yet winning second place didn't discourage young Shea; it only served to whet his appetite for the new medium. He was hooked. He took voice lessons from an instructor who had an office on top of the old Met building. He also practiced the piano and even tried his hand at writing. Yet, though he earned a spot singing popular music on NBC with Allen and impressed the critics and scores of fans, he still didn't feel he had discovered a direction for his life. Although he was viewed as a catch-miss talent, he was not so sure. This son of a minister felt as though he should be doing more.

"One Sunday morning in 1933 Mother placed a beautiful poem on the piano of our home," Shea recalled. "It was written by Rhea F. Miller. I know that Mother put it there so I would see it. She obviously wanted me to read the words. I had a habit of going to the piano the first thing every morning, so I immediately saw the poem. As I studied the words I was overcome with emotion.

"Upon reading it over, a second verse just hit me," Shea remembered. "I began playing in the key of B flat and just started singing the poem. I didn't know Mother was in the next room having her Sunday morning devotional. I didn't know anyone could hear me. I just sang the song the way it was given to me."

Shea's mother was overwhelmed. She thought the music her son had added to the poem had made "I'd Rather Have Jesus" one of the most powerful songs she had ever heard. She encouraged him to sing it during his father's service that day. While many others in their congregation were also moved by this new work, Shea didn't do anything about publishing the song. He and the song weren't ready just yet.

A couple of years later, Shea moved to Chicago and auditioned for a spot on a CBS program that originated there. When he failed to get the job, he began to question if the Lord really had any plans for him to use his voice. Those doubts were quickly forgotten when the president of the Moody Bible Institute asked him to sing religious music on the school's daily radio program. Desperately needing a steady job, the now-married Shea accepted the offer and began performing with the program *Hymns From the Chapel.*

"Christian music brought new dedication and purpose in my life," Shea explained. "I was really being blessed through my work. I had been singing on the show for about two years when a young Bible student named Billy Graham introduced himself to me. He just wanted to tell me how much he enjoyed my songs."

Over the course of the next decade Shea received countless offers to leave the hymn-centered program and sing on bigger shows. The only catch was that he would be asked to perform popular music on these outlets. He graciously turned down all the offers. He was now convinced he had received a call to reach lost souls by using his musical talents. He left the Moody program when he took a job as the singer and host of a national ABC radio show dedicated to Christian music. He stayed with the network and the program until Billy Graham reentered his life and asked him to provide the special music for the Graham crusades. Although he knew it was an enormous financial risk to leave an established broadcast home for the revival circuit, he did it anyway. He had once been convinced that God wanted him to sing only Christian music. Now he was just as convinced that God wanted him to work with this dynamic young man.

In the years just after World War II the Billy Graham Crusades began to draw nationwide attention. In huge tents the evangelist preached night after night to ever-growing throngs. Soon the crusades were picked up by radio and then a new medium, television. Graham's charisma was so strong that the tents soon had to be folded and replaced by large arenas and stadiums. And the crowds continued to grow larger.

Shea's solos set the tone for the preacher's messages. With his full, rich baritone, Shea not only charmed audiences, he also touched them with the message of each song he chose. Yet night after night the song that seemed to make the biggest impact was "I'd Rather Have Jesus." When he sang that he would "rather have Jesus than men's applause" and "worldwide fame," people sensed that he meant it. They believed him.

RCA signed Shea to a recording contract and captured his talent in their studios. The song that the company chose to initially spotlight their new singer was "I'd Rather Have Jesus." Thanks to the record, millions who had never heard Billy Graham or been to a crusade of any kind could now hear and be moved by Shea's dynamic rendering of a song inspired by a poem found on a piano. The man who turned down a chance to be a pop singer because he believed the Lord had a better purpose for his voice now found himself more popular than most of the famous secular singers of the day.

Six decades after he first matched his music with Rhea Miller's words, George Beverly Shea is still singing "I'd Rather Have Jesus." Everywhere he goes people still turn out to hear this message in music. The singer usually deflects the credit for this song's mighty impact to the writer of the poem. Yet in truth, while the message of the song is a mighty testament in itself, what has made this song so special and such a powerful force in the Christian world is that Shea has not only sung the lyrics, he has lived them. Everything he stands for is reflected in each line of his signature song.

If That Isn't Love

Reading the titles of Dottie Rambo's classic gospel songs is like reviewing a list of gospel music's greatest hits. Ms. Rambo has written more than two thousand Christian songs, including "I Will Glory in the Cross," "I Just Came to Talk with You, Lord," "Build My Mansion Next Door to Jesus," "We Shall Behold Him," "Sheltered in the Arms of God," and "He Looked Beyond My Fault and Saw My Need." Her musical testimonies have been recorded by many singers from Elvis Presley to Bill Gaither. As a songwriter, she has been called the Queen of Gospel Music, and there are few who will even argue the legitimacy of this honorary title. Dottie's personal impact on the world of gospel music has been almost as incredible as her output of original compositions. Not only one of the industry's most beloved figures, she is also one of gospel music's best role models.

The fact that Dottie apparently writes her music with ease belies not only the hard work she puts into her craft but also the heartaches and cruel experiences that often led to her inspiration. In spite of her obvious talents, when she was a child her father refused to allow her to study music, perform in church, or speak out about her faith. At a time when most teenagers were thinking about proms and planning graduation parties, Dottie had been married for two years and had a baby. When she and her husband Buck accepted a call to full-time Christian service, they sacrificed any hope of financial security, traveled constantly, and gave up the stability of an easy, normal existence. Yet Dottie never looked back, never questioned her call, and never doubted her faith.

After she had risen to the top of her field, Dottie didn't have much time to enjoy the acclaim she received. Plagued by health problems and all but crippled by back trauma, she seemed to linger on her deathbed several times only to rebound and come back with a renewed faith and an even more powerful testimony. Never complaining, constantly lifting others up to Christ, the physically frail Dottie had an inner strength that would put the muscles of Sylvester Stallone's Rambo to shame. Through incredible highs and lows, this soft-spoken yet dynamic woman has become an icon of how to completely serve the Lord with talent, faith, and praise.

The wonderful story behind "He Looked Beyond My Fault and Saw My Need" is told earlier in this book. Yet this song cannot be separated from another of her most beloved efforts. As Dottie's need to find a way to lead her dying brother to the Lord inspired "He Looked Beyond My Fault," Eddy's acceptance of Christ as his Savior and his death soon after led to Dottie's writing a bookend tribute to her Lord.

For Dottie Rambo, as for most other songwriters, moments of great triumph or tragedy often bring about inspiration to create a story in music. Many writers have enthusiastically penned words of praise based on a miraculous recovery or a great revival. Songs such as "He Touched Me" and "I Saw the Light" were created in moments of joy and optimism. Other writers have dealt with death, despair, and heartache in pieces like "Farther Along" and "Where Could I Go but to the Lord." Yet rarely do these great highs and lows come together into one composition. Few writers have the genius to mix these opposite emotions in a single inspired work.

For years before she wrote "He Looked Beyond My Fault," Dottie Rambo had been carrying around a heavy burden of despair caused by her brother's eager and willing jump into a life filled with sin. Yet when Eddy came to accept Christ as his Savior, Dottie's soul was suddenly filled with indescribable joy. Eddy's salvation was the answer to years of long prayers, and it lifted the burden of worry from her heart.

Yet within weeks of his acceptance of Jesus, Eddy died. His death and the reality of Dottie's never again being able to share in his life on earth were very difficult for her. It was very hard to say a good-bye to a loved one who now seemed to have so many reasons to live. Caught in a strange mix of emotions, Dottie thought back to some of the final words she had shared with Eddy. They had talked a great deal about the fullness of God's love. In her brother's mind, Christ's forgiving and saving him proved that His love knew no bounds.

By using Eddy's story of a life of sin followed by a single act of forgiveness, coupled with her own new understanding of suffering and death, Dottie wrote one of the most profound descriptions of God's love ever written.

Focusing on the picture of Christ dying a horrible and lonely death for each of us, Dottie used the theme "If that isn't love, then what is?"

Although "If That Isn't Love" was written as a very personal testimony, everyone who has heard it has seemed to claim it as their own. Recorded countless times, it became a standard not only in gospel music but in country and pop circles as well. Recorded by choirs, quartets, trios, duets, and solo artists, it swept into churches, was placed in scores of hymnals, and was used at both weddings and funerals. As few other songs had ever done, it defined *agape* love.

As long as Dottie Rambo lives on this earth, she will never be able to visit with her brother. As long as she lives, she will probably also never completely escape the pain that has been caused by her own numerous health problems. Yet, though she misses Eddy and longs to walk effortlessly on stage to share her music with others, she still uses the love that fills her heart and comes out so wonderfully in her songs to inspire and heal others. Dottie has given the world so much joy and inspiration for so long that no one would blame her if she retired and stayed at home. Yet in spite of the effort it takes because of her back problems, she continues to write, sing, and give her testimony. It is no wonder that when her peers look at the sum total of her Christian life and witness, they often say, "If that isn't love!"

If We Never Meet Again

There are only a few special moments for even the best songwriters when great inspiration and universal appeal come together in a single work. Perhaps no other gospel composer, except possibly Bill and Gloria Gaither, ever experienced more of those special moments than Albert Brumley. His ability to match emotions with lyrics was unfathomable. In three short stanzas Brumley could preach some of the greatest sermons ever heard. Best of all, those who listened to his inspirational messages usually left singing them as well. Thus, even when the master was gone, his thoughts were still touching lost souls through the voices of others. No one can comprehend how many people Albert led to the Lord through his work, and now, even years after his death, the master scribe is still touching millions each year through his songs.

For most of his adult life, Albert traveled a great deal. In old tabernacles, brush arbors, churches, auditoriums, theaters, and stadiums, he not only sang but also taught others to read music, sing harmony, and write songs. By the time of his death he had been recognized as a giant in his field, yet the journey had not been an easy one. Brumley had worked his way up the ladder of success one rung at a time. He had struggled for years. Perhaps this is the reason that even during his days of greatest acclaim, he lingered to meet every man, woman, and child who had come to his performances. He wanted to do more than thank them, he wanted to look into their hearts, feel their needs, share their joy, and get to know their individuality. It was from these one-on-one meetings that Brumley drew much of the inspiration for his work.

Perhaps better than any other person, Brumley knew the sad reality of meeting, making ties, and then moving on. As time passed and as the many meetings and venues that sought him began one after another to crowd his schedule, Albert realized that the new friends he made each night would probably never have a chance to see him again. The thought of not being able to share a song, a story, or a meal with these people began to weigh heavily on his mind. How he wished he could come back in a year, gather the same group around him, and find out what heartaches and blessings had come into their lives.

"Dad recognized when he was traveling with and singing with groups," Albert Brumley's sonr related, "that the same crowd would never be together. He realized that many of the people who had made each gathering so special would never again be in the same place at the same time. Being a very sentimental man, the thought of not being able to meet with men and women who had quickly become such dear friends made him sad."

When World War II broke out, this realization of the transitoriness of relationships grew worse. Albert couldn't look into a crowd without seeing the faces of young men he knew would soon be fighting for their lives on a distant battlefield. Beside them he saw sweethearts who would soon know the anguish of uncertain separation. Not far away there were the images of mothers and fathers wondering if their sons would be struck down by an enemy's bullet.

As the United States entered the war and as more and more boys and men boarded ships and planes headed for uncertain futures, Brumley's thoughts of separation, thoughts of his never having another reunion with each new group, and the very realization that many in each crowd would soon die began to haunt the eternally optimistic Brumley. *Why was life so fragile?* He questioned. *Why were there no words to calm anxious souls?*

In the midst of the war, Albert was driven to sit down with pen in hand and try to put into words the emotions of his heart. Surprisingly, the words came easily. With very little visible effort, Brumley wrote three stanzas and a chorus. Arranged for family four-part harmony, his newest composition—the outpouring of a heart overcome with a sense of loss—quickly became an anthem of faith for millions during the war.

Brumley never considered himself a master of high art. He never thought of his verses as ranking with the works of Shakespeare or Mark Twain. Yet set to simple melodies and arrangements, his lyrics spoke to the hearts of both rich and poor. Men and women who were on a spiritual quest found answers in his text. Many who had never even considered coming to the Lord met Him for the first time in an Albert Brumley composition.

During World War II his song "If We Never Meet Again" brought solace and comfort to a nation at war. Yet even after the fighting had ended and most of the sons, husbands, and fathers had come home to their families, the song continued to provide a lifeline for those who had lost loved ones. It remains so very popular even today because it is more about life than death, about coming together rather than being apart. "If We Never Meet Again" is Christian faith taken to a higher level of understanding by three simple stanzas and a gentle chorus.

I Know Who Holds Tomorrow

$\mathcal{E}$ven the greatest Christians are often dealt cruel blows by the world. Accepting Jesus as one's Savior does not assure one of a life free from tragedy. Ira Stanphill, whose great songs have inspired men and women for more than half a century, was a committed man who knew pain and suffering first hand. He was also a Christian who was tempted to compromise his own principles and to put his needs ahead of the Lord's.

Stanphill's first wife left him for a life filled with adulterous relationships and bouts with addictions. When the couple divorced, his ex-wife took their only child. Everywhere he went there were whispers, rumors, and lies all around. Many people pointed fingers. Some felt he should leave Christian work because of the shame of his divorce.

Yet Stanphill was not at fault. It was not he who had given up. He had remained true to his vows. It was his wife who had broken her wedding vows. He had forgiven her and tried to rebuild the union again and again. Yet in spite of these facts, Stanphill didn't explain his own innocence. Rather than speak of what had gone wrong, he let it be known that he intended to keep his wedding vows no matter what the cost.

In the late forties, Stanphill was working at the Bethel Temple in Dallas. The church, one of the largest in the South, was well known across the nation as the home of the Stamps School of Music. Because of the church's dynamic ministry and the school, Bethel was a fertile environment for spiritual growth. Yet at the very moment Stanphill was surrounded by some of the greatest musical talents he had ever known, he was not collaborating or producing great new works. Rather, he was feeling sorry for himself.

He had recently met a young woman who he knew could be the love of his life. She seemed to be perfect for him. She loved music, children, and God. She was a dynamic Christian whose charisma drew others to her beliefs. Ira felt Gloria loved him as deeply as he loved her. Yet he had made her very aware of the fact that he couldn't marry again. He had even urged her to find someone else.

Stanphill determined to forget Gloria and to focus instead on his music. Yet even as he did, her image consumed his thoughts. He began to think of her so much that he feared she was taking the place of God in his life.

More than once he considered breaking his solemn marriage vow. He knew that no one would blame him for it. After all, his ex-wife had been with several men and was singing in night clubs. She was living in sin. Who would criticize him for not being true to her now? Yet every time he came close to accepting his own rationalization, he realized that though the world might forgive, he would never forgive himself for putting his own wishes ahead of his vow before God.

One morning, while driving to his office at Bethel Temple, he began to talk out loud to God. He wanted to know why he had to give up on love in order to continue his Christian service. It just didn't seem fair. As he continued to plead his case before the Lord, he felt increasingly sorry for himself. He was faced with two alternatives: do the right thing and spend his life alone and in misery or do what he felt was wrong, give up his Christian work, marry the woman he wanted, and spend the rest of his life living with the guilt. He could accept neither road. His life seemed hopeless. As he sank deeper into depression, he began to hum a tune. Soon he was singing a song about not knowing what was in the future, but realizing God was walking with him every step of the way.

Stanphill was so moved by the thought of God taking every painful step with him that when he arrived at work he rushed to a piano and quickly finished writing "I Know Who Holds Tomorrow." Although he couldn't understand why, he suddenly felt at peace. He knew he could go on with his work. Everything would be all right, because God would take care of his needs.

"I Know Who Holds Tomorrow" is one of the greatest testimonies of faith ever written. In the framework of very simple lyrics, Ira Stanphill admitted he didn't understand why bad things happen to good people, why Christians make mistakes, and why people have to suffer in their daily lives. And even after acknowledging that there was much he didn't know, he joyously discovered the one truth he could be sure of—he knew who would hold tomorrow.

"I Know Who Holds Tomorrow" has been recorded countless times. It is one of the most familiar gospel music selections played on radio and sung in churches. Just recently country teenage superstar LeeAnn Rimes used it as a focal point for her best-selling Christian album. Yet what makes this song so very special is not only its message but also what happened in Ira Stanphill's own life after he wrote it.

He didn't break his vow, he didn't compromise his beliefs, he stayed true to his word, and he remained right with God. Yet he also married the woman whose love had challenged his commitment to Christian service.

A few months after Ira finished the final stanza to "I Know Who Holds Tomorrow," his first wife died in a car accident. Soon after he and his son had begun to build a new life for themselves, Gloria crossed their paths again. A few months later, as Ira's bride walked down the aisle, he really understood that the Lord not only holds tomorrow but also rewards those whose faith is strong enough to forgo the temptations of today.

Ira Stanphill may have been just trying to answer his own questions about faith when he wrote "I Know Who Holds Tomorrow." Yet fifty years later it seems that his personal message of hope and service is timeless and speaks to the hearts of every Christian.

I'll Fly Away

In 1927 Albert E. Brumley had achieved a lifelong dream—
he was studying at the Hartford Musical Institute under the
tutelage of gospel music's legendary songwriter and publisher,
Eugene M. Bartlett. During his first year of formal musical
training, the Oklahoma farm boy plunged deeply into his studies. He tried to learn as much as he could about every facet of
songwriting and music theory. As the spring semester drew to
a close, a joyful Albert revealed the fruits of a year of learning
to his teacher and classmates in the form of a song he had been
led to compose. The nineteen-year-old was justifiably proud of
"I Can Hear Them Singing Over There." He thought he had
used the tools of his education coupled with his own Christian
experiences to write a song worthy of publication. Yet long
before his first hymn found a publisher, it was greeted by a
loud chorus of critics.

The other students at Hartford felt Albert had simply
copied E.M. Bartlett's old material and had not come up with
anything new. They declared that rather than be considered a
songwriter, he should be labeled a plagiarist. Albert was deeply
hurt. He had not knowingly copied any song. While "I Can
Hear Them Singing Over There" might have reminded others
of Bartlett's work, it was only because Bartlett had made such
an impact on the young man's life. Even though Albert
attempted to show the steps he took in writing his song, no one
was ready to listen. It seemed that he had been found guilty

without a chance to prove he possessed the talent to write a solid gospel song on his own.

Packing his bags, Albert left Arkansas and went back to his parents' farm. When it came time to return to school for the fall semester, he didn't pick up his suitcase and head for the train station; rather, he grabbed a hoe and walked to the cotton fields. Yet this attempt to distance himself from those who had ridiculed him would pave his way back to respect in the eyes of his fellow Hartford students and change his life forever.

One day, while out in the field, Albert began to sing one of the nation's most popular hits, "The Prisoner Song." As he thought of the hopelessness of spending a life behind walls, with no chance of escape or parole, he began to really understand life as a prisoner. Stepping out of himself for a moment, the young man could see the concrete barriers and the guard towers and feel the chains around his leg. For an instant he was a prisoner, and the song was his story.

When he finished singing "The Prisoner Song," Albert allowed his mind to come back to the field. As he walked the long rows in silence, he began to think of how much he disliked the hard life of a farmer. Noting a bird soaring high in the afternoon sky, he wished for an instant he could be that bird and fly far away from the drudgery that was now filling each day.

By the time he finished his afternoon in the field, Brumley had begun to turn the concept of "The Prisoner Song" into the framework for a religious piece. Using his own thoughts of a bird flying off to a better place, Albert titled his new effort "I'll Fly Away." Yet trying to weave the imagery he saw in his mind into a hymn did not come easily. For months only the song's skeleton held the writer's inspiration together. Even after he returned to study at the Hartford Institute in 1929, "I'll Fly Away" was little more than a title.

For the next few years Albert not only studied with E.M. Bartlett, he worked for him too. Singing with the Hartford Quartet, Brumley traveled throughout the South selling songbooks and magazines for his employer. By the middle of the Depression, he had become the top man in Bartlett's organization and was making $15.00 a week.

Now married, Brumley badly needed the money, so he continued to sing and travel for Hartford. Yet his passion to write drove him to pull out "I'll Fly Away" from time to time. In 1936, when he finally became satisfied with the song, he sang it for his wife, Goldie. She encouraged him to publish it. When he took "I'll Fly Away" to his boss, Bartlett was also impressed. The publisher placed the song in one of the company's new books. It quickly became the Hartford Publishing Company's favorite offering.

Having a song that was being recorded countless times and selling thousands of copies of sheet music should have put Albert in a position to break off from Bartlett and go out on his own. He should have been able to afford to write full time. Yet when he had signed the contract giving him a weekly salary, he had also signed a clause giving the publisher all rights to anything he created. So while "I'll Fly Away" did establish him as a songwriter, it did nothing for his financial state.

Ironically, it was Brumley's first song, the one that had been so widely ridiculed by his fellow students, that first purchased him some freedom. Coupled with the status of "I'll Fly Away," "I Can Hear Them Singing Over There" allowed Brumley to break out on his own, form his own publishing group, and begin writing full time. Although still a close friend of E.M. Bartlett, and still more than happy to go on the road from time to time with the Hartford Quartet, Brumley relished the freedom to create his own Christian music. Although he was no longer bound by a contract, he was still bound by reality. Many days he found himself out in the hot sun laboring in a field or running down a stray cow. But even though he was publishing a lot of his music, he still wasn't free to fly away and give his life completely to his work. He still had to farm to make ends meet.

Over the next few years Brumley composed more than six hundred songs. Many, such as "Turn Your Radio On," "I'll Meet You in the Morning," "If We Never Meet Again" and "I Just Steal Away and Pray," anchored a gospel explosion that took this once largely rural American music around the world. Although he would later earn the title of the "World's Most Recorded Songwriter," none of his many wonderful songs would ever reach the level of popularity or recognition of "I'll Fly Away." None could purchase the kind of freedom and security that that song could give.

During World War II, E.M. Bartlett suffered a stroke and slowly wasted away. Brumley often made the long trip to visit his fallen hero. In Bartlett's bedroom the two men swapped stories, shared laughs, and talked about the blessings each of them had known. Not once did Albert ask for rights to his song, never did he question the contract that had cost him so dearly.

Not long after Bartlett's death, Brumley discovered that the rights to "I'll Fly Away" had been given back to him. A last act of kindness and the hundreds of thousands of dollars in royalties that came with it, paved the way for Albert Brumley to finally have complete security and be able to fully give his life to his music and his Lord. Thanks to E.M. Bartlett, Albert Brumley finally was free to soar like a bird.

In the Garden

C. Austin Miles grew up in a church community and once considered giving his life in Christian service, but instead surrendered to a calling in pharmacology. Although he often worked long hours, in what spare time he could find he continued to read the Bible and lead singing in his church; he also tried his hand at writing songs. After years of perfecting his composing craft to the extent that he felt comfortable sharing his work with others, Miles sought out a publisher. It was a move that would not only dramatically alter his life but eventually touch millions of hearts as well. Hall-Mack Publishing offered the young man a contract on his first songwriting effort and, impressed with his abilities, hired him as an editor. For the remainder of his life Miles was closely tied to the business of Christian music publishing.

In 1912, when Miles was forty-six years old and had spent many years with Hall-Mack, his boss, Dr. Adam Geibel, asked him to come into his office. Geibel felt the company needed a song that was sympathetic in tone, breathed tenderness in every line, and brought faith to those whose hopes had been crushed by the problems of life. Unable to complete the project himself, Geibel asked Miles to try his hand at writing such a song.

Weeks later, as the last gray vestiges of March shone through his study window, Miles spent a portion of one of his free days taking and printing photographs. An accomplished photographer, he was often amazed at the things he saw for the first time when looking at an image in a darkroom. He had often first noted only in a print the deep texture of a scene, the shadows on a wall, a flower all but hidden by underbrush, and a thousand other things he had missed when he had first framed the shot with his camera. On this day it was no different. In the black and white images he printed, the very ones he had recently composed, he saw detail he didn't realize had been there.

No doubt inspired by what had been revealed in the photos, Miles sat down at his desk and began to think of the assignment his publisher had given him. Unable to define a theme, much less come up with a melody or verse, the writer put down his pencil and picked up his Bible. For the next several moments he studied the twentieth chapter of John. When he came to the text telling of Mary, Peter, and John visiting the tomb, he leaned back in his chair and imagined himself going through that same garden to visit the final resting place of the crucified Savior. As he took that walk to the tomb, he found himself awash in imagery. What would it have been like to have gone there alone and found a risen Lord, he wondered. Picking up his pencil, he scribbled down the scenes that were developing in mind. He didn't look up until he had completed the text for a poem he called "In the Garden."

As a photographer Miles knew it took time for a picture to develop. Thus, even though he had the words in hand, he didn't immediately rush to the piano to match his lyrics to music. Instead, he set his copy aside and joined his family for supper. It was hours later, long after darkness had replaced daylight and a cold wind had driven people off the streets and into their homes, that he began his search for music to go with his verses. It took only a few moments for the melody to his new song to fall into place.

Geibel was impressed with Miles' work. As he listened to "In the Garden" for the first time, he was all but moved to tears.

Never had his instructions been followed so dramatically. Not only had his writer given him a song to fill a void in the company catalog, but Miles had brought out images even he had never considered when he had been working with the original concept.

Hall-Mack rushed the song to publication and soon licensed it to scores of other music publishers around the world. Almost a decade later, thanks in no small part to the advent of radio, "In the Garden" became one of the best-known early American gospel songs in the world. Although written on assignment and inspired from a single man's experience of reading Scripture, "In the Garden" seems to speak to everyone who hears it. With beautiful words linked to a timeless sweet melody, the song effortlessly fits every era, every musical genre, and every person who sings it. As one sees something new in a photograph or painting each time he picks it up, so it is with the song each time it is heard or sung.

Austin Miles died in 1946. During his almost eighty years on earth he sang in hundreds of churches, gave thousands of music lessons, and edited countless songs. Yet his signature work always remained this one song. With "In the Garden" Miles provided millions with a lasting anchor of faith through a picture developed as he himself had walked in a garden with Christ. This picture not only came to define the writer's own life but also touched millions of people for his Lord as well.

I Saw the Light

Of all the performers who have made their marks on the country charts, Hank Williams stands apart. In his brief six-year recording career he touched more hearts and won more fans than any other musician of his era. He was an original. Hank was like no one who had come before. He was a common person from a humble background who was elevated by a special God-given talent that he used to transform his own confused and haunting life by producing music that was suffused with subtle yet profound messages.

As one listens to the music of Hank Williams one quickly understands that he was in touch with millions of Americans' hearts. Yet Hank never was able to find his own soul. He played under the brightest spotlights while roaming the darkest streets. He was country music's king, but he was also a lost pauper.

An alcoholic who seemed to be able to give up drinking for only a few days at time, Hank's genius stood out even during his deepest depression. There can be no doubt he was self-destructive, but he was also wonderfully gifted. His music was so profound in story and song that it has long outlived him, and through his mix of gospel, blues, and country, as well as his embracing of the sounds and soul of black rural music, he shaped every form of music, including country-gospel, for generations. By putting all of his great pain and his few joys into his music, he found a pipeline of understanding to his millions of fans. In a very real sense he became to American folk music what Mark Twain is to American literature. No one could turn a phrase as he could. No one could paint the word pictures he painted. No one could compose such simple but awe-inspiring melodies. And no one could do it as often or as quickly as Hank.

With songs like "I'm So Lonesome, I Could Cry," "Your Cheating Heart," "I Can't Help It If I'm Still in Love With You," and "Cold, Cold Heart," Hank Williams became a country music legend even while he drank his life away. Yet in the midst of showing up for appointments drunk and forgetting the words to his greatest hits in concerts, on radio, and at live shows, Williams always devoted a part of his program to gospel music. With songs like "Mansion Over the Hilltop," he stepped back from the pain of his life and sang of the hope of a life beyond—a life with the Savior.

Williams penned a song that quickly found its way into churches and all-night singings: the classic country-gospel ode, "I Saw the Light." In his own unsophisticated manner, he wrote the story of a man who had wandered in darkness, blinded by sin and despair, then, when he had discovered Jesus, was changed so dramatically that he now lived in the light.

"I Saw the Light" became the song that Williams always used toclose his shows. For a man who seemed to live in an ongoing state of depression and continually wrote of sadness and gloom, "I Saw the Light" gave his shows the upbeat posture that breathed optimism into his final bow. For his fans, his friends, and his peers, "Light" gave hope that "Old Hank" would turn the song into his personal testimony.

Yet much like the tormented literary giant Edgar Allan Poe, Hank Williams seemed possessed by demonic forces that kept pulling him out of the light and into the depths of darkness and shadows. It was there, in the hopeless mire of booze and pills, that Hank usually sought refuge from the demons only he saw and understood. The only clue as to what Williams experienced while fighting in the gutter for his soul was the anguish of the words of his songs. No one song ever summed up Hank's view on his own life better than "I'm So Lonesome I Could Cry." Critics have called it the saddest song ever written. It probably is.

Hank's creations, such as "I'm So Lonesome I Could Cry," not only proved his genius, but also usually confirmed his nightmares. He was looking for happiness, love, and acceptance, and they were right in front of him, yet he constantly chose the bottle over the Bible, the bad over good, the dark over the light.

By the age of twenty-nine Hank was a used-up, worn-out shell of the enthusiastic young country idol he had once been. His face now resembled a death mask, his skin wrinkled, his manner slow, his gait a bit unsteady. People who had met him just a few years before, now scarcely recognized him. Those around him seemed to sense that he was heading down a road that led straight to hell, but they were at a loss as to how to stop him.

Even as his rapid downhill spiral continued, Hank continued to write classic country songs, and he continued to sing "I Saw the Light" at the end of each of his shows. Smiling a forced smile, Hank would then wave to the crowd and rush to a waiting car to take another hit from a bottle of booze. One evening, as he repeated this routine for the hundredth time, he turned to another country music star, Minnie Pearl, and sadly shook his head. As the city lights bathed his face in haunting shadows, he moaned, "That's the problem, Minnie, there just ain't no light."

Those words haunted Minnie Pearl when, a few weeks later, on January 1, 1953, she was told that Hank Williams had died of a heart attack on the way to a show. Like so many others, Minnie never knew if her friend found the light he had written about in his song.

At the small theater where fans had gathered to hear Hank sing, the news of his death was at first greeted by cold silence. Then, one by one, the crowd stood up and began to sing, "I Saw the Light." It was more a prayer than a tribute.

"I Saw the Light" is now not only a country classic, but a gospel classic as well. With the exception of "Amazing Grace," perhaps no gospel song is known by more people. For millions "Light" is a wonderful example of the power of salvation. For many others who have used this song as a means to help them escape alcoholism, drug addiction, and depression, "I Saw the Light" represents a real beacon of hope.

It may seem ironic that one of America's best-loved gospel songs was written by a man who couldn't find the light in his own life. Yet for the many sinners who have understood not only the message of "I Saw the Light" but also the writer's pain, it seems only natural that a man struggling in darkness was inspired to write about the hope, freedom, and light that were just out of reach.

We can pray that Hank Williams found the light before he died. We can hope that he embraced the Savior he knew in his mind but couldn't embrace with his heart. But in reality we cannot be sure of Hank's decision until we reach heaven. Until that time we will just have to live by the hope of which he wrote and celebrate that so many others who have heard "I Saw the Light" brought that Light into their own hearts and lives.

It Is No Secret

Stuart Hamblen was born in Kellyville, Texas, on October 20, 1908, the son of a preacher. As a young child he often traveled with his father from church to church on horseback, listening to both Bible stories and tales of the Old West. It was the latter that grabbed his soul, and by the mid-twenties Stuart was making his living as a cowboy singer in Dallas. In 1928, he migrated to the East Coast, was discovered by the Victor Talking Machine Company, and had recorded what proved to be the first of hundreds of records.

After making a name for himself in New York, Stuart caught a ride to Los Angeles and, thanks in part to his record deal and easy-going manner, quickly became a local favorite. It was a national pop hit, "Texas Plains," a song he wrote, that assured him a solid place in Hollywood. By the mid-thirties he was working as an actor and singer in motion pictures, had married a beautiful starlet, had his own radio show, and was a popular guest at all the studio parties.

For the next fifteen years Hamblen lived the fast life, drinking, gambling, and staying up all night partying with friends. He also continued to write and record top hits such as "Little Old Rag Doll," "Golden River," and "Brown-Eyed Texas Rose." With an ever-growing bank account, he flew through the Great Depression and World War II in style. He had a nice home, drove the best cars, and ate at the finest restaurants in town. Yet even as he became more and more popular, he found himself more lonely too.

After a time, his wife, Suzy, grew tired of Stuart's star-crossed lifestyle. Turning to God, she gave her soul to Christ and began a decade-long effort to convince Stuart to slow down and think about what he was doing to his body and soul. Suzy's pleas and prayers seemed to have little effect on him. He spent far more time at the racetracks and bars than he did wondering about his own eternal fate. Any other woman might have figured he was a lost cause, but Suzy was too much in love with her husband to give up on him. In the face of years of broken promises and rejection, she continued to pray for a miracle.

One morning a young evangelist and his featured singer were guests on Hamblen's radio program, called *Sawdust Trail*: Billy Graham and George Beverly Shea. The three swapped stories, spoke of Graham's upcoming revival meetings, and sang a few songs. When the two guests parted from their amiable host, few figured they would ever chance to meet again. Yet for reasons not even Hamblen could understand, he felt drawn to Graham and Shea—so drawn that he decided to check out their "act" in person.

In 1949, when Billy Graham had come to Los Angeles to conduct revival services, most of the entertainment empire was skeptical of the preacher. When he asked people to turn out for nightly Christian meetings and sit on unreserved and uncomfortable folding chairs in an old circus tent at the corner of Washington and Hill, most predicted the preacher wouldn't survive long in a town that was a-glitter with modernity and prosperity. Largely in jest, newspapers christened Graham's tent the Canvas Cathedral, and thousands who drove by the portable church each day laughed at the thought of finding God in such a shabby environment. Yet as the weeks passed, many of Hollywood's elite became curious enough to turn out. One of those stars who decided to join a few friends under the big tent was Stuart Hamblen.

In truth, Stuart might have been the life of almost every party, but even he had come to realize there was a huge void in his life that couldn't be filled by alcohol. Although he had found fame and fortune, he felt empty, unworthy of his wife's love and devotion and all the blessings that had come his way. Although his drinking pals might have scoffed at the notion that he could find something of value in an evangelist's message, the songwriter/actor decided to give up partying for one night in order to hear what the "other side" had to offer.

The atmosphere, the music, and the message probably reminded Hamblen of the days of his youth. Yet for a reason even he couldn't explain, he was now understanding the meaning of being a Christian for the very first time. He felt the reality of the Lord not only in his head but also in his heart. Overcome with emotion, with Suzy by his side, he came forward at the invitation and accepted Christ as his Savior.

Hamblen's decision quickly became the talk of the town. Everyone who had worked with him on radio, bought his records, and acted with him in cowboy movies wondered about it. As he walked away from the party scene and as he gave up his once-cherished drinking and gambling, even the most jaded could see that a powerful change had come over the man.

One sunny day Stuart was strolling down a Hollywood street when he ran into an old friend—John Wayne. The two exchanged handshakes and greetings; then Wayne observed in a wry voice, "Hey, I heard about what happened to you."

Smiling and shaking his head, Stuart replied, "I guess it's no secret."

Laughing, the film giant responded, "That sounds like a song to me."

For the next few minutes John Wayne and Stuart Hamblen walked side by side with Stuart explaining the way he felt, what it meant to have the Lord in his life, and the goals he now had for the future.

"You know, John," he said, "what God has done for me, He can do for you."

The meeting with John Wayne haunted Hamblen. Deep into the night he reflected on their visit. Buried in thought, he was snapped back to reality only when he heard his mantel clock strike midnight. Quickly picking up a piece of paper, he scribbled the words, "The chimes ring out the news that another day is through. . . ." Well before dawn Hamblen had polished those words and finished composing what would become his own personal testimony.

As a way of presenting the new Stuart Hamblen to the world, the radio host recorded and released "It Is No Secret" in 1951. The single took off on both pop and country charts. It jumped into popular music's top forty and hit #3 on the country and western playlists. Most importantly, it paved the way for Stuart to become one of the nation's most respected Christian voices.

Before he died in 1989, Hamblen had written a host of other great gospel songs that were recorded by countless inspirational and secular artists. Not satisfied to simply set his own faith to music, he also became a Christian speaker, appearing at thousands of church meetings, rallies, and crusades. It has even been said that he led John Wayne to the Lord.

"It Is No Secret" has evolved into more than just one man's testimony. Millions who have never heard the writer's name can identify with the promise of his song. Simple and direct, Stuart Hamblen's message clearly spells out the Lord's invitation and promise to everyone who accepts His will for their lives.

I Wouldn't Take Nothing for My Journey Now

In the late 1940s a brother-and-sister team made up of Howard and Gussie Mae Goodman began to sing at small Alabama churches. Within just a few years the family duet had grown to include siblings Stella, Ruth, Sam, Rusty, and Bob, as well as Howard's new bride, Vestal. With their rural sound and country harmonies, the Goodmans were a favorite at many of the Assembly of God churches in the area surrounding their home. Yet as the family's members began to grow up, marry, and find jobs, the group started to fall apart. About the time Rusty began a hitch in the service and Howard and Vestal moved to Kentucky to devote their lives to pastoring a small church, rural Alabama lost the unique sounds of this family.

When Rusty's tour of duty was up, he landed in Baton Rouge, Louisiana, and began to work with various musical groups. For several years he toured with country acts, tried his hand at writing secular songs, signed a publishing agreement with Louisiana's former governor and nationally known singer Jimmie Davis, and struggled to make ends meet. Now married and a father, Rusty's lust for fame during these early days of rock and roll simply couldn't be satisfied. He seemed unable to get a break. Yet that didn't keep him from trying, and as he strove for the top, he also fell away from the strict moral life he had known as a child.

By the late fifties Rusty's career was completely stalled. Trying to find peace and happiness, he attended a service at the First Assembly of God Church in Baton Rouge. Overcome with a sense of renewal, he met with the pastor, was baptized again, and felt the Lord leading him to the Kentucky home of his brother and sister-in-law.

"On an early Saturday morning," Rick Goodman, Rusty's nephew, remembered, "a car horn blew. Howard opened the parsonage door, and there was a U-haul trailer, packed heavy with family goods. Standing beside the old car and trailer was Rusty, his daughter Tanya—she must have been about five or six—and his wife. He didn't know what he was going to do for a living, how he was going to support his family, or where he was going to live. Yet even though he was confounded and confused, what was obvious was that he was happy."

The small church where Howard preached had a new organ, and though Rusty didn't know a thing about the instrument, he began to try to play it. Within just a few minutes of sitting down at the console, he had written a song, "The Answer Is on the Way." Governor Davis's company published that first gospel composition and mailed Rusty a check for $1,200 for all rights. The money, as well as the publisher's encouragement, was just what Rusty needed. Soon he was working with the choir, writing other gospel songs, and going with his brother Howard to camp meetings to both sing and preach. Joined by brother Sam and Vestal, the Goodman quartet soon became known as the Happy Goodmans.

Certainly there was never a better name for a group. Not only were the Goodmans obviously happy to be singing in front of people, but their up-tempo style of gospel music seemed to make everyone who heard them happy too. In their singing there was a sense of joy that was heartfelt. A great deal of that emotion must have come first of all from the knowledge that the Lord had reclaimed Rusty and also that this had been instrumental in bringing the family back together in song.

"Rusty was writing a great deal during his first months back," Rick recalled, "and his songs were being used not only by the family but by our choir too."

Even though the Happy Goodmans were getting more opportunities to sing and even though Rusty had written some wonderful new songs, what the group didn't yet have and what they really needed to expand their ministry was a special song that would define their message, their spirit, and their unique sound. The inspiration for this song came from a very unlikely source.

"There was a little man in our town," Rick Goodman explained. "He was a small man whom everyone called Brother Shorty Carter. Shorty didn't belong to just one church; rather, from Sunday to Sunday he visited all the churches in the area—a different one every week. It didn't make any difference if it was our church or the Baptist or Methodist, at some point he would raise his hand during the service and ask to testify. Because he was retarded and was looked upon as a misfit, most preachers would ignore Brother Shorty and just go on with their sermons. But not Howard. He would stop the service and let Shorty testify. We all knew that Shorty wouldn't make much sense, but we also knew that it would only take about two minutes for him to share what was on his heart. This went on for years, and always, just before he would finish his testimony and sit back down in his pew, he would say, 'You know, I wouldn't take nuthin' for my journey now.' He always said it the same way."

Not long after Rusty Goodman had moved back to rejoin his family, Shorty Carter had a stroke. When Howard received the news, he rushed to the hospital. The little man was very weak, drawn, and close to death. Yet when the preacher walked in, Shorty nodded his head and smiled, feebly waving Howard over to his bed. This man who had lived on the edge of poverty, had been made fun of by almost everyone he had met, and had been pitied and shunned could have been expected to be bitter. Shorty could have been expected to have cursed his life and his final fate. Yet as Howard leaned over to hear his last words, Shorty Carter whispered, "I wouldn't take nuthin' for my journey now."

Inspired by Carter's words and attitude, Rusty Goodman sat down and wrote "I Wouldn't Take Nothing for My Journey Now." When he finished his work, he knew it was not only a perfect song for the Happy Goodmans, but a wonderful tribute to Shorty Carter.

"Rusty sent the song to Jimmie Davis," Rick explained. "Jimmie paid him $2,000 for it, but that was for all rights. So when it was published, it had Jimmie's name on the song as the writer. That was just the way the business was back then, and people accepted it. The important thing to Rusty was that he had some money to support his family and that Shorty's message was out there being heard."

The Goodmans premiered "I Wouldn't Take Nothing" on a Tennessee Ernie Ford PBS special. Soon after that they recorded it, using Nashville's best producer, Owen Bradley, along with the best country session players they could find. Placed on their second album, the song came out before the Goodmans became gospel music sensations, so it wasn't an immediate hit. Yet as the Happy Goodmans' fame grew and as their sound became not only recognized but also loved, "I Wouldn't Take Nothing" surfaced as their signature song. A decade after Rusty had written it, it was one of the most recognizable pieces in southern gospel music.

In 1990, his body all but consumed by cancer, Rusty Goodman was forced to quit singing with his family. Although still a young man, his days were numbered, the disease had progressed too far to be treated. Yet just like the little man who had once inspired him, Rusty didn't give up, didn't grow bitter, and didn't ask, "Why me?" Even at the end, when pain racked his body, Rusty still made it clear that he wouldn't take anything for the journey he had been given.

Today, whenever it is performed, "I Wouldn't Take Nothing" always brings smiles, shouts of joy, and applause. The song now considered a piece of gospel music's rich fabric, new contemporary groups are putting their spin on it. As countless others hear the wonderful testimony that can be found in the lyrics of this classic, it proves again that God can use even the humblest among us to reveal His message. Shorty Carter's testimony, which once hardly anyone in a tiny Kentucky town wanted to take the time to hear, has now been heard by millions!

Jesus Loves Me

The very first Christian song most children learn is "Jesus Loves Me." If there was a best-seller hit list among the preschoolers, this very simple but precious song would have to be at the top of the charts. Yet few people know that "Jesus Loves Me" began life not as a song but as a part of one of 1860's best-selling novels.

Anna Warner was well aware of the coming of the war between the states. She lived with her father and sister on Constitution Island. Their home was practically next door to the United States Military Academy at West Point, and from her front porch she constantly heard the rumors of war. Yet even in the face of uncertain times, every Sunday Anna taught Bible classes to the cadets. She realized that if the southern states made good on their threat to withdraw from the Union many of the boys she knew could be killed or wounded in the war that would follow. While it broke her heart to consider the dismal fate for those too young to have experienced the many blessings of life, she also fully comprehended the importance of leading each of them to Jesus now. With an urgency brought about by a nation on the brink of dividing, sharing Christ's love became her mission in life.

Besides her teaching, the forty-year-old Anna also wrote. With her sister Susan she had written several novels, using the pseudonym Amy Lothrop. In 1860 the sisters' *Say and Seal* became the country's best-selling work of fiction. Written for the masses and the moment, not fueled by timeless struggles or epic writing, the book would quickly pass from the public's fancy, lost with thousands of other period pieces of the time. Yet, thanks to one very special scene on but a single page, the essence of the book and of Anna's faith would live for decades after *Say and Seal* and Anna herself had been forgotten.

In one chapter a child lay dying. Nothing could be done to ease his pain or give him a second chance at life. As his ultimate fate grew nearer, the novel's focal character, Mr. Linden, attempted to comfort the small boy. Looking into the child's eyes, he slowly recited a poem that began, "Jesus loves me, this I know, for the Bible tells me so."

The words of the poem made the boy's last moments of life much easier. These simple lines also moved thousands of readers to tears. Hauntingly beautiful, composed straight from Anna's faithful heart, "Jesus Loves Me" quickly sprang out of her book's pages and became one of the most beloved poems of the era. No one can even begin to calculate how many times it was said on the battlefield, in the homes of children whose fathers were engaged in the Civil War, from pulpits and in Sunday school classes, and even at the White House itself. Ringing so clear and true, Anna's sixteen short sentences had touched the hearts of millions with verses meant only to calm the soul of a dying fictional character.

One of the scores of readers who memorized the poem was William Bradbury. A teacher of voice and organ, in 1854 Bradbury had formed a piano company with Ferdinand Lighte and Henry Newton. Besides heading up his business, the noted musician also continued a practice of setting his faith to music by composing his own songs. By the beginning of the Civil War, Bradbury had built his own music company to publish and distribute his works. It was during the time when his music business was taking off that he first read and fell in love with "Jesus Loves Me."

Although an accomplished composer of what many think of as high-church music—he had already lent his talents to such hymns as "Sweet Hour of Prayer," "He Leadeth Me," and "On Christ the Solid Rock I Stand"—Bradbury was moved in a much different fashion when he decided to add a melody to Anna Warner's poem. A lover of children's voices, as well as a proponent of music education in both school and church, Bradbury allowed the child in his own heart to spring forth when writing the simple musical notes for "Jesus Loves Me." Then, to fully complete the work, he added the following chorus:

Yes, Jesus loves me,
Yes, Jesus loves me,
Yes, Jesus loves me,
The Bible tells me so.

The marriage of Warner's words and Bradbury's music was one of the most beautiful gospel efforts of all time. Yet the song "Jesus Loves Me" might have been as quickly forgotten as the novel *Say and Seal* if Bradbury's music company hadn't published it. Through the publisher's established distribution network the new children's song quickly worked its way across the North and South. In the face of the most horrible fighting this nation had ever known, both sides were singing about a Savior who died, yet had risen and still watched over everyone with equal love and compassion. It was an ironic message for a very ironic time.

Almost a hundred and forty years after this song was first published, few know of the writings of Anna Warner or recognize the name of William Bradbury. But even though the writer and the composer have been forgotten, everyone knows their song. Children and adults of all races and even millions outside the Christian faith can sing "Jesus Loves Me." How many millions have clung to this message on lonely nights or rocked babies to sleep while singing this song is unknown. But what can be most assuredly stated is that "Jesus Loves Me" is the foundation on which many children not only first come to know Christian music but also come to know the love and sacrifice of the Lord who inspired it. And this message is what keeps them singing the gospel throughout their lives.

Just a Closer Walk With Thee

"Just a Closer Walk With Thee" is one of the best-known gospel songs in the world. Its words are a reflection of the message of the New Testament, but its theme is as old as the children of Israel. It has been recorded countless times by scores of artists in a wide variety of gospel and secular genres. Everyone from the Blackwood Brothers to Mahalia Jackson have lent their talents to these simple lyrics and tune. It is now so much a part of the American worship experience that it has found its way into hundreds of hymnals.

Most people associate "Just a Closer Walk With Thee" with the Reverend Thomas A. Dorsey. The words and music do seem to reflect Dorsey's masterful blend found in "Precious Lord, Take My Hand," yet rather than coming from the pen of the father of gospel music, "Closer Walk" probably influenced his style. By the time Dorsey began writing his own inspirational songs, choirs had been singing "Just a Closer Walk With Thee" for generations.

Although first popularized during World War II, the song seems to date back before the Civil War. Personal histories jotted down by African-Americans of the late 1800's and 1900's mention slaves singing as they worked in the fields a song about walking by the Lord's side. It is not surprising that one could trace the popular classic's roots back more than a hundred years before its mass introduction to the American public.

Many of the themes of gospel music come from early African-American history. Christian slaves often took the ideas and concepts of the religion they found in this country and melded them with the music and rhythms of their ancestral home to make a rich blend that spoke to their particular situation. The result of this musical and theological marriage is now known as the Negro Spiritual. This rich fabric of oppression and faith probably gave birth to "Just a Closer Walk With Thee."

Over the course of the next hundred years "Closer Walk" was passed down from generation to generation, from church choir to church choir, remaining a staple of the southern black religious experience. Yet it wasn't until the 1930s, when black churches banded together to create massive musical conferences, rallies, and conventions, that "Just a Closer Walk With Thee" found a national audience.

In her book *We'll Understand It Better By and By*, Bernice Johnson Reagon documents the fact that pioneer gospel songwriter and arranger Kenneth Morris heard noted vocalist William Hurse sing "Just a Closer Walk With Thee" in a 1940 concert. Copying the words and researching the song's history, Morris determined that it had never been published. Creating additional lyrics and a choral arrangement, he released the song in printed form just months after first hearing it. By 1941 the song had already risen to become one of the most popular African-American church anthems. Not copyrighted and therefore a part of the public domain, other publishers, including Stamps-Baxter, also quickly picked up the song. Thanks to radio performances by numerous versions of the Stamps Quartets, "Just a Closer Walk With Thee" had become a white quartet favorite by the end of the war.

Although steeped in black history, the song was quickly adopted by southern whites as their own. Its rural feel, its simple and direct message, even its musical chord pattern, seemed to reflect the popular country music of the era. So it should not be surprising that in 1950 Red Foley took his version of the spiritual to #9 on *Billboard*'s country music charts. In the mid-fifties Elvis Presley released it as a part of an extended-play 45 RPM single and set sales records for this format that have never been broken. By 1960 Tennessee Ernie Ford had established "Just a Closer Walk With Thee" again as a gospel hit. A decade later more than a hundred artists had recorded the song, making it a classic.

Even though the song has become one of the most universally performed and recorded gospel songs, because it is still very much a personal prayer set to music, many men and women seem to grasp this classic as their own. The song's lyrics seem to echo individual needs, thus making it the perfect inspiration for times when faith has reached a low ebb.

> *I am weak, but thou art strong,*
> *Jesus, keep me from all wrong,*
> *I'll be satisfied as long*
> *As I walk, let me walk close to thee.*

Born in slave fields, created by an unknown writer who knew well the chains of a cruel and unfair world, nurtured by a people whose hope for a better life could be met only by the help of a loving Savior, "Just a Closer Walk With Thee" is now a universally accepted and loved gospel song that has transcended race, culture, and time. The song has become a classic because of its message. To find God, people must understand and accept their own fragility—they must humble themselves to come to know and love Him, and they must come to rely on Him so that they can have His strength in even the most oppressing times.

Just a closer walk with thee,
Grant it Jesus if you please,
Daily walking close with thee,
Let it be, dear Lord, let it be.

This has been the plea of many throughout the centuries. It was the plea of the slaves working the fields of the American South, of the disciples left to carry on the work after Jesus' crucifixion, as well as of every man and woman who has been through hard times, has been deserted, or has lost health or strength. The writer of "Just a Closer Walk With Thee" knew doubt and pain, but he also understood faith.

Just a Little Talk With Jesus

$\mathcal{A}$ miracle meeting happened on a bitterly cold 1977 Tennessee day, the kind of day when the wind seems to whip right through one's clothes. Sylvia Mays, who worked at a small Nashville publishing office, figured that few folks would walk in off the streets trying to sell songs on this frigid January morning. She fully expected to be able to catch up on the paperwork that had built up over the holidays. She was caught completely by surprise when she heard a door opening and a man's voice inquiring as to what kind of songs Canaanland Music published.

As Sylvia observed the two visitors approaching her desk, she couldn't help but note how out of place they looked. Most of the songwriters who ventured into Canaanland were young idealists. They were often dreamers who hadn't lived long enough to understand just how tough the music business really was; they were usually fresh-faced and innocent. The man who was speaking to her now looked as if he had already reached the age to apply for Social Security.

"I have written some songs," the finely dressed, dark-skinned man began, "and I am looking for a publisher."

Sylvia heard those words many times each day. In most cases she took a tape, got an address, offered no guarantees, and then wished the writers well. She fully expected to do the same this time too. As the man continued to speak, Mays got ready to give her prepared speech.

"I live in Washington D.C.," he continued, "and I believe that I have written some songs a gospel music publisher might be interested in."

When she got a chance to cut in, Sylvia politely inquired, "Have you ever had anything published before now?"

Smiling, his dark eyes lighting up to her question, the man replied, "As a matter of fact, I have even had a few recorded."

Surprised, Mays followed up his response by asking, "Would I know any of them?"

Not pausing for a second, the old man answered, "Have you ever heard of a song called 'Just a Little Talk With Jesus'? I wrote that and some others, too."

Sylvia stared at her guest for a moment, then queried, "What is your name, sir?"

"I am Cleavant Derricks, but most people call me Rev."

Asking the gentleman to be seated, Mays hurried to her phone to call her boss.

"It was the most incredible experience in my life," recalled record producer Aaron Brown. "I can remember it vividly. I was away from my office at a recording studio and Sylvia Mays called me at the studio. She told me an old black man had just walked in and was claiming he wrote 'Just a Little Talk With Jesus.' She thought that he was very convincing, but she wasn't sure if he really was who he said he was. I didn't know what to make of it. I thought Cleavant Derricks was dead. Yet Sylvia convinced me to leave the studio and come back to the office. By the time I was able to get away from the studio and back to the office, the men had been waiting for two hours.

"Even after I shook his hand, I still wasn't convinced this was really Cleavant Derricks. I took him into my office and tried to find out some more about him. I think he realized he had to convince me that he was who he said he was. It seemed strange that it apparently didn't bother him a bit."

"I wonder if you would let me sing for you," Derricks asked of Brown. Then the old man, using no accompaniment, began to lean sideways and sing the lead. When he came to bass lines, he would lean the other way and hit them. By the end of the first stanza both Mays and Brown knew they were in the presence of a legend.

"I remember I started crying," Brown explained. "He was really freaking me out. We spent the rest of the day together and he told me his story."

That story was one of both inspiration and heartache. Derricks had written a host of great gospel songs in the middle of the Depression. "Just a Little Talk With Jesus," like most of the others he had penned, was a song meant to lift the spirits of the poor people who were members of his Alabama church. While he had sensed that his songs were special to his friends and parishioners, he never dreamed others might find comfort in his words too. Yet encouraged by those around him, he made a long journey to Dallas to meet with the men who ran the company that supplied the songbooks for his rural church.

At the Stamps-Baxter Publishing Company in Dallas, Texas, Derricks had been received like most other writers of the time. The owners politely listened to his work, looking for a hidden gem. They liked "Just a Little Talk With Jesus" and asked the writer what he wanted in return for the publishing rights. A deal was struck, and the preacher left Dallas with fifty new songbooks for his church. For that small price the publisher gained all rights for two of his songs. Although happy at the time, the writer soon discovered that the deal was not unlike the one the Indians got when they traded Manhattan Island for a trunkload of beads. By 1940 "Just a

Little Talk With Jesus" had become one of America's most beloved gospel standards and was one of the hottest songs in the Stamps-Baxter catalog.

"Over the next few months after that meeting in my office," Brown recalled, "I got to know the Rev. well. As a matter of fact I fell in love with him and wanted to help him. So I tried to help him get back some of his royalty rights. I told his story to Francis Preston, the vice president of BMI, and she convinced BMI to give him back royalties for the past six years and establish him as the writer for all future songs. He immediately received fourteen thousand dollars. He had never seen that much money at one time in his life.

"After we made that deal, a few months passed, and he moved to Knoxville. We were now close friends, and so I wasn't surprised when he called me and told me he wanted me to meet his family. A few days after that call he came to Nashville with his wife, his twin sons, his daughter, and cousin. They wanted to sing for me. When I heard them, I could have run through a wall. They were great! I immediately signed them to a record contract. In the studio, as we were cutting many of his unpublished songs, I happened to ask if he wanted to sing 'Just a Little Talk With Jesus.' It was only then that I discovered that one of the greatest writers and song stylists in gospel music history had never cut his greatest work."

Cleavant Derricks's 1977 vocal version of "Just a Little Talk With Jesus" would prove to be an unforgettable recording and a very special moment in gospel music history as well. When the Rev. sang his song, his voice grew rich with expression, tears streamed down his face, and his hand pointed to the heavens. In his voice and his eyes everyone in the studio could read a lifetime of Christian service and faith now realized in a single defining moment.

Cleavant Derricks died not long after cutting his most beloved composition. Yet the inspiration that first lifted the spirits of his small rural congregation and grew to touch millions around the world lives on in his work and still brings comfort to countless souls. Most gratifying for Aaron Brown is not the money generated for his company, the countless new artists who have married their talents to "Just a Little Talk With Jesus," or even the myriad of new choral arrangements of the song; rather, it is the fact that the Rev.'s faith, spelled out so clearly in this song's lyrics, was proved when his song was given back to him and his family. Just as he had promised his congregation when he sang his most beloved song for the first time, with faith every wrong can be made right.

Keep on the Sunny Side of Life

In the late 1800s, Ada Blenkhorn was often given the job of taking care of her nephew. The boy had been crippled in an accident, and because of his injuries he missed out on a great deal of the joy and wonder of being a child. Usually trapped at home with very little to do, he found in Ada a beacon of hope and understanding. On pleasant days she often took him out of the house in his wheelchair so he could see the wonders of God's world.

The trips along the streets where he lived were something the boy always looked forward to. He didn't care much where he went or what he and his Aunt Ada saw, and he didn't complain about how long or how short their sight-seeing tours were; in all of her years of pushing him, he had only one request: "Please, Aunt Ada," he would beg, "just keep me on the sunny side of the street."

For months Ada Blenkhorn responded to his plea to stay in the sunshine. When she pushed him in the bright rays of warmth, she noted the way his eyes sparkled and his face lit up with joy. If he could have walked, she just knew that in the golden light of the morning sun she would have seen a spring in his step.

After completing one of their trips down the sunny side of the street, Ada returned home and scribbled down a poem. Using her nephew's one desire coupled with her own Christian faith, she quickly jotted down a chorus and three stanzas for "Keep on the Sunny Side of Life." Set to a tune composed by J. Howard Entwisle, Ada's "Sunny Side" slowly worked its way across the South via all-night singings and revival meetings.

It is doubtful that this very early gospel effort would ever have become nationally known if it had not come to the attention of a southern music teacher named Laish Carter. He not only taught it to his pupils, he also took it home and taught it to his family.

Laish's brother A.P. Carter had formed a family music group that performed at local churches, schools, and dances. Called the Carter family, the trio consisted of A.P., his wife Sara, and A.P.'s sister-in-law, Maybelle. With A.P. singing bass, Sara the lead, and Maybelle adding harmonies, by 1926 the family was well known around their home community of Maces Springs, Virginia. Sensing there was money to be made in the entertainment business, the Carters became one of the few rural acts to search for bookings that paid real money.

In 1927 A.P. overheard the news of Victor Talking Machine record scout Ralph Peer's arrival in Bristol, Tennessee. A.P. was determined to drive the twenty-five miles for the audition and not to leave until he had heard his family's voices on a recording.

When the country family arrived and introduced themselves, the New York scout must have been amused. Dressed in their finest, the Carters nevertheless looked like something out of a Mark Twain short story—"country" in every sense of the word. As they sat down to perform, Maybelle was so far along in her pregnancy that she could barely hold her guitar. Still, out of courtesy, Peer gave them a fair shot. Ultimately, this shot would become a musical movement heard around the world.

Sara Carter was a raw and untrained singer, but her phrasing and emotional tone set her apart from all others Peer had ever heard. Because she styled lyrics, Sara was distinctive in a world where most rural female singers sounded alike. In spite of her pregnancy, Maybelle was a talented instrumentalist who brought a whole new style of play to both the autoharp and the guitar. Her unique method of picking the chords on the low strings with her thumb while playing the lead on the high strings with her fingers created a musical sound Peer had never heard before. Only now do historians realize that it was on Maybelle's rhythm that country music was built. And then there was A.P.

It was the two women who made the Carter music unique, but it was A.P.'s insight and drive that fueled the team. A.P. Carter was a promoter, a booker, a public relations man, and a salesman. Even if the Carters' singing hadn't sold Peer on them, A.P.'s sales pitch probably would have. He seemed to know everything about folk music. He had transcribed hundreds of folk songs, old hymns, poems, and country jigs. He had taken scores of primitive lyrics and melodies and refined them, shaping them into something that had commercial value. One of the songs A.P. had refined and that the Carters sang for Ralph Peer was "Keep on the Sunny Side of Life."

In the spring of 1928 the Carters made a trip to the Victor Studios in Camden, New Jersey, and recorded Bleukhorn's song. Released in October, the single jumped onto the nation's top-ten list. Although the song and the Carters were hardly what was being played on radio stations of the day, "Keep on the Sunny Side" remained one of popular music's hottest-selling songs into 1929. Other acts recorded it, but "Sunny Side" became so identified with the Carter Family that they used it as their theme song for the next decade.

Even though the Carter Family eventually was included in the Country Music Hall of Fame, most of the several hundred songs they recorded were forgotten by the time A.P. died in 1960. Yet, along with "Wildwood Flower" and "Can the Circle Be Unbroken," "Keep on the Sunny Side" continued to be sung and recorded. Even today the simple song inspired by a crippled boy's desire to feel the sun shining on his face remains a staple of rural country gospel meetings.

"Keep on the Sunny Side of Life" is nearing a hundred years of age, but it wears those years well. While most other folk-oriented gospel songs have faded from memory, this one has continued to be learned and played. The reason for the continued acceptance of "Sunny Side" has to be its message. The song is about a message of faith promised in the New Testament—the faith brought by Christ to a dark world.

Etched on A.P. Carter's tombstone are his name, dates of birth and death, and a record. With the scores of hits the Carters had during their four decades of work, one might wonder which one would be picked to sum up A.P.'s remarkable life. It was not a song he wrote and not a song he discovered, but rather it was his personal favorite that best summed up what Carter viewed as the secret to a happy life—"Keep on the Sunny Side of Life."

The King Is Coming

$\mathcal{I}$ remember vividly the first time I ever heard a live rendition of "The King Is Coming." I was a college student, sitting in a Fort Worth, Texas, auditorium, listening to the *Battle of Song*. Some of the nation's greatest gospel groups had gathered to share their music with the thousands who had filled the Will Rogers Coliseum. Although I enjoyed the whole evening, there was one moment when time stopped. At that instant, with no warning, as if hit by lightning, I was magically transported to a vision of a glorious future. It was as clear as any image I had ever seen. The musical vehicle that so moved me was written by my generation's greatest inspirational songwriters and delivered by one of gospel music's most important families. It was a marriage of song and artist that seemed ordained in heaven, and perhaps it was.

Tom Speer had grown up on a southern farm. A lover of music, he used to sing traditional gospel and folk songs while following mules in the fields. With the limited training that pre-radio days offered, Tom somehow grew from singer to music teacher, eventually working for one of the most important publishers of gospel music, the Stamps-Baxter Company. During this same time Tom and his brother Brock joined two other men and sang gospel music throughout the South. In 1921, when Brock left to work full time in publishing, Tom added a woman to the ensemble, and the Speer Quartet was on its way to becoming one of the best-known pioneer southern gospel groups. That first female voice, Lena Claborn, later married

Tom and began a family of vocalists who are still performing today. For almost eight decades, the Speers have not only sung gospel music but have also lived it every day of their lives.

Although they began as a traditional male group, it was the mixture of male and female voices that made the Speers unique and gave them a very special identity. As the years went by and as they relied more heavily on true family harmonies, their sound became much tighter than that of other quartets of the era. By the thirties, Tom "Pop" Speer and Lena "Mom" Speer had been joined by their children—Brock, Rosa Nell, Mary, Tom, and Ben. Thanks to radio and a constant travel schedule, the Speers became one of gospel's best-known families.

Perhaps because of their children and their evolving tastes, the Speer Family embraced new musical styles and influences much more quickly than most other southern gospel quartets. They weren't afraid of change and weren't put off by new ideas and sounds. By World War II many churches had even stopped hiring the family because their style had become too jazzy and modern. Contemporary long before the word was used to describe the hot Christian groups of the seventies, the Speers respected tradition but knew how to push the envelope to continue growing and expanding as performers, evangelists, and Christians. Perhaps that is why they stayed fresh for so long and were able to move audiences with the latest, very nontraditional offering by Bill and Gloria Gaither.

"The King Is Coming" represented a major departure not only from the gospel music of the era but also from the music the Gaithers were writing during the late sixties. Born out of evangelist Jim Crabtree's sermon on the joy of the Second Coming, "The King Is Coming" had more of the feel of an anthem than a southern gospel singalong. It would be hard to imagine it in a shaped-note hymnal. It was much different from other

Gaither works such as "He Touched Me" and set the tone for many more modern efforts that followed, including "God Gave the Song."

Performed with blasting trumpets, surging organs, and booming choirlike harmonies, this incredible vision of a day even many Christians avoid thinking about fired imaginations in a way few songs ever had. More powerful than any religious tract, deeper in scope than most sermons, Gloria's words and Bill's music painted a vivid picture of the day when a triumphant Christ will return to claim His people.

"Previously I had tended to think of the end of the world as a time of judgment," Gloria later explained, "but that day I thought of all the beautiful endings to people's life stories that Satan had tried—but failed—to ruin. I thought of Jesus as the Master of restoration—of marriages He had put back together, relationships His hand had mended, and generation gaps His Spirit had bridged. I saw an image of the coronation of a King who walked down the corridor of history; I could see lining the corridor throngs of witnesses to His redeeming grace."

For millions of Christians "The King Is Coming" was the most moving song they had ever heard. Beginning with a scene where "the marketplace is empty" and ending with a choir singing "Amazing Grace," this Christian musical presentation containeed more drama in a few short lines than did any Cecil B. DeMille three-hour Hollywood epic. On the night I first heard the Speers present it, as well as on thousands of other nights in countless other places, "The King Is Coming" brought people to their feet, completely consuming their thoughts of the world's greatest reunion.

"When the lyric was written," Gloria later wrote, "I felt spent, yet shaky with excitement. I took the words to Bill, and he immediately played and sang them, fitting them like a glove to the music he'd been hearing in his mind. His chorus finished the piece with simplicity and power."

Bill and Gloria Gaither's music has usually dealt with the joy of living a Christian life. Their songs have been testimonies of daily faith. Yet in "The King Is Coming" they not only departed from their usual style but also offered a new vision that few had ever considered, much less imagined. Thousands of historians and theologians have written and spoken of the Second Coming, scores of artists have tried to paint it, but nothing has ever presented the picture so clearly and so wonderfully as "The King Is Coming."

Life's Railway to Heaven

Since the dawning of Christianity, walking the straight and narrow has been a rule every person of faith has tried to follow. In verse, song, and story, following the footsteps of Jesus has been the one sure way of staying in touch with one's faith and being a good witness to others. Yet all who have tried following Jesus have stumbled, and all have fallen short. No one has managed to avoid all the temptations along their way.

The last half of the 1800s were revolutionary times in the United States. It seemed that the Civil War and the opening of the West had led to a period when lawlessness and immorality were rampant. Children grew up idolizing the likes of outlaws such as Jesse James and Billy the Kid. In many communities a saloon had replaced the church as the central meeting place. The nation had been forced by law to come back together after a bloody war won by forces of the Union, yet people remained divided even while living under one flag. Even Christian denominations broke into separate groups over issues such as slavery. These were days of division and immorality. Many pastors and politicians of the time thought America would never again adhere to the rule of the straight-and-narrow path to salvation.

In 1890 a Baptist preacher by the name of M.E. Abbey saw order in the chaos. While others were predicting doom and damnation, he sensed that the nation he so loved was coming back together. In his mind this was not an immoral time of hopelessness but an era of great potential for spreading the gospel and reuniting with friends and family. The reason he saw such promise had to do with the expansion of the railroad.

Abbey thought of the railroad as a door of opportunity. He thought that in much the same way as freight and passengers could be shipped over the rails, faith could be delivered as well. It thrilled him to realize that rail service had made the United States smaller and was bringing more and more people together. If enough Christians just made an effort to take their faith with them as they moved from station to station, then the story of Jesus would soon be heard by everyone.

No doubt a great deal of Abbey's optimism came from railroad men he had met. He knew several engineers who were devoted men of faith. He had watched them take their Christian compassion along with them on the rails. He had seen them become role models to the children who idolized the men who drove the big locomotives. Abbey had himself seen these men praying, teaching, and reaching out. He had also observed the great responsibility they felt in keeping their passengers safe. It was these Christian men, not only handling millions of tons of steel through their skills but touching hearts as well, who gave the preacher confidence that America was turning a corner of faith. They also inspired him to write a poem, using a train and an engineer as his focal point.

Upon first glance, "Life's Railway to Heaven" seems almost childlike in its simplicity. Yet upon further review these lyrics embrace a subject as complex as life itself. In the four stanzas and the chorus of his poem, Abbey used the imagery of a long rail journey to illustrate the way to live a Christian life. In parable form, he pointed out life's many pitfalls and the need to keep the faith, to keep trusting in the Lord, and to realize the joy of finally reaching home and sharing in the rewards that await the Christian there.

Abbey's poem might have been lost to all but his congregations if he hadn't given a copy to Charles Tillman. Tillman, a songwriter, took the preacher's words home to Atlanta, sat down at his organ, and composed a melody for them. Then together he and Abbey found a publisher. Long before the advent of radio, the song was a hit. Sheet music sold into the hundreds of thousands of copies, and many popular singers of the day cut it during the dawning of the age of recorded music. As Abbey had figured, Americans still did have a thirst for matters of faith. Faith just had to be packaged in a way a new generation could understand.

"Life's Railway to Heaven" was one of the first successful gospel songs to use both real-life points of reference and popular music to "sell" its message. Although quickly adopted and adapted for Christian hymnals, "Life's Railway to Heaven," except for its theme of faith, had more in common with "The Ballad of Casey Jones" or "Wreck of the Old 97" than with the great hymns of the time. Abbey, who saw a changing world and progress as paths of opportunity, also helped create a new type of religious song. Using modern reference points to teach old truths, the preacher touched millions who otherwise might never have made the connection between the lives they were living and their Savior, much less made the final connection between here and the hereafter.

Mansion Over the Hilltop

There was a great deal to be happy about in 1945. The war that had cost more than thirty million lives was over, peace had brought about a renewed enthusiasm and optimism, and millions of families were being reunited for the first time in years. It was a time of homecoming, rededication, and rebirth.

Yet even in the midst of the celebration of peace, there were many who were incredibly sad, too. As they saw all the servicemen coming back to civilian life and as they watched them at train stations and airports, they were reminded of the fathers, husbands, and brothers who would not be coming home. These men had given the ultimate sacrifice for their country and all that was left now for their families were old photos and fading memories.

These mixed emotions hovered over a late-summer evangelism service in Dallas conducted by the Reverend Gene Martin. In his audience were hundreds of reunited families looking for renewal alongside many other families mourning the loss of loved ones and looking for answers. Also in the service was Ira Stanphill, one of the most celebrated gospel music composers of the period.

That evening the services were capped by a local businessman who spoke to the crowd about his memories of the recent Great Depression. Stanphill quickly learned that this man had been wealthy when the stock market had crashed in 1929. He had been on top of the world, only to see that world fall apart beneath him. Slowly, as the years dragged by and the economy failed to rally, this man saw his business grow smaller and smaller. He had to let many of his most valued employees go, move out of his large home, and cut corners at every juncture. Still, with nothing more that he could do to "downsize," his situation grew even worse.

As a Christian he began to wonder about his own faith. He began to question God. He even began to doubt if the Lord cared about him at all. Each day he found himself deeper in debt. Each day he was confronted by fewer customers and larger bills. Each night he was haunted by nightmares. Each morning he wondered if he shouldn't just close up and join the bread lines.

One day, when he was at the lowest point in his life, he left his office and pointed his car down a highway. He didn't have a destination point, didn't look at a map, and cared little about the passing of time. He simply drove until he felt the urge to turn onto another road, then he drove some more. Hours after he left Dallas, he found himself on a rural dirt road filled with pot holes, littered with trash, and devoid of any vestiges of urban civilization. His car labored as it crossed the deep ruts and traversed the rolling hills. Hopelessly lost, unable to turn around on the narrow trail, he pushed on, finally coming to an old house that seemed as though it had been abandoned years before. To his surprise, as he pulled into the lane overgrown with grass and weeds, a small child came wandering out of the shack and walked up to his vehicle.

How can anyone live like this? the man wondered. *How can they face life?* Yet the child who came to his car wore a huge smile. The doll she carried was broken, the clothes she wore were ragged hand-me-downs, and her home was little more than a clapboard shanty, but it appeared that she was unaware of her poverty. It seemed to him that this child was as happy as any person he had ever met.

Overcome with curiosity, the depressed businessman asked her how she could be so happy living in a such a dire state of poverty. Her answer was that someday her father was going to build a nice house up over the hill and she was looking forward to that time.

The child's optimism about the future reenergized the man's spirits. After bidding the girl farewell, he turned his car around and headed home with a renewed faith. Although it would take a great deal more struggle and several years of work, his business eventually rebounded. His livelihood restored, he rehired past employees and once again lived without fear and worry about what would happen in the future.

In the audience, many people shouted "Amen" as the man finished his testimony. Yet Ira Stanphill was not as moved by his story of surviving the Depression as he was by the little girl's faith in her father to give her all she needed. Seizing that concept, he went back to his home and sat down at the piano. In one sitting he composed "Mansion Over the Hilltop."

When Stanphill finished fine-tuning his song, his simple verses reflected not only the businessman's testimony and the little girl's faith but the message of Christ as well. Rather than dwelling on stockpiling worldly treasures, rather than measuring ourselves against the success of others, rather than coveting things we don't have, we can have a new vision through the message of "Mansion Over the Hilltop." The song spoke of a man who had little wealth on earth but knew the Lord had prepared a home for him in heaven that was greater than any he could imagine.

The song's simple melody and lyrics were easy to learn, and many felt this was the reason the song became an immediate hit in gospel music. But more than this, coming at the end of World War II when so many Christians had lost family members in the fighting, this beautiful song of faith and heaven also offered comfort and hope to millions. For many who questioned why a loved one's life and unlimited potential had been cut short, "Mansion Over the Hilltop" was the crutch that got them through each day.

It is said that music is the universal language. In gospel music this is probably most true. The stories that come from the soul, the songs that are inspired by real-life examples of faith and loss, stand apart not just for a few, but for almost everyone. Ira Stanphill's "Mansion Over the Hilltop" is more than a song; for millions it is a promise that not only makes life on earth a bit easier but also makes the next life that much more appealing. Yet what this special song really represents is child-like faith. With that faith, nothing is impossible.

Milky White Way

In the thirties and forties one of black gospel music's premier quartet singers was Landers Coleman. Coleman not only provided excellent vocals and wonderful arrangements to the groups he sang with, but he also penned some incredible songs. Of all of Landers' inspired compositions, there was one that not only stood out in 1945 but continues to guide listeners to the heavens today.

Landers Coleman had to have been inspired by a clear night sky when he composed "Milky White Way." The song's simple theme portrayed a single soul climbing up to heaven via a staircase in the stars. This thought may seem farfetched, but it is no more so than the image of riding to glory on a train or in an airship, and both of those vehicles had been used in several famous inspirational songs of the time. Besides, the story of Jesus' resurrection did indeed speak of rising into the air, which is a great deal like the spirited imagery used by this writer.

When Coleman composed "Milky White Way," he had recently buried loved ones. He missed them and desperately wanted to see them again. Not understanding even a small portion of God's mystery and only grudgingly accepting the fact that many of his close friends had died tragically, Coleman found both comfort and joy in picturing the time when he would not only see his mother again but also be able to ask God about all the things he couldn't comprehend now.

Although the song's spiritual feel and vivid descriptions set it apart from most gospel standards of the period, if "Milky

White Way" had not found its way to a rising Baltimore Quartet, it is doubtful that Landers' best work would have become widely recognized.

By the mid-forties the Trumpeters were one of the best-known African-American gospel quartets on the East Coast. Over time their arrangement of Landers Coleman's "Milky White Way" became their most requested song at tent meetings, gospel conventions, and all-night singings. In 1947 the Trumpeters cut their arrangement of the tune and it shot to the top of the black gospel playlists, even crossing over to become a hit on R&B and pop playlists.

What made the Trumpeters' version of "Milky White Way" so special was the lead vocal work of Joseph Armstrong. Armstrong simply let the Spirit guide him as he rode the notes. He dipped into refrains by singing out words like "well, well, well," actually speaking quick bursts of lyrics, then blending with the other three vocalists on refrains. True, this recording of Armstrong and the Trumpeters was little more than an arrangement of "Milky White Way" created in live performance. To the group and the people who loved them this was not unusual. This is how almost all black artists performed gospel music. Yet for many of the white audiences who heard the record, the spontaneity of this black performance was something brand new.

Up until this song, most of the African-American–inspired gospel classics that had made their way into southern white gospel had been "cleaned-up." This process had eliminated much of the freedom of movement that had given the music its life and spirit. So when the Trumpeters' version of "Milky White Way" made its way onto the pop charts, white audiences were suddenly awakened to a sound that seemed as fresh as a spring breeze. This not only opened new doors of opportunity for many black artists in once-segregated music circles, but it also allowed many white groups to use the less structured arrangements that had driven black spiritual music for more than a century.

Thanks in large part to "Milky White Way," the Trumpeters became one of the most popular African-American quartets in the nation. They were such a draw that the CBS radio network approached them about hosting their own gospel music radio show each morning. They agreed, and throughout the late forties and early fifties the Trumpeters introduced the swinging, free-feel black gospel music to an ever larger audience. Naturally, "Milky White Way" was their theme song. For millions this song signaled the beginning of a show that featured the very best sounds in gospel music.

"Milky White Way" remains important today for two reasons: (1) Landers Coleman painted wonderful and joyous pictures of faith with his lyrics, and (2) this song helped open the door for the acceptance of African-American interpretations of gospel music. Even today Landers Coleman's song still presents a beautiful map to the stars.

My Tribute

$\mathcal{P}$erhaps there has never been a gospel music writer who is more in demand by mainstream entertainers than Andraé Crouch. Although he has written scores of gospel classics such as "Soon and Very Soon," "Through It All," and "My Tribute," as well as spend most of the last thirty years reaching millions by performing at churches and Christian concert venues, everyone from Vanessa Williams to Diana Ross to Paul Simon has sought him out for advice. The winner of eight Grammy Awards and an entertainer who has performed in almost sixty different countries and is as well known in Japan as he is in the United States, Andraé Crouch *is* gospel music to countless fans. Yet he is much more than that.

When Steven Spielberg filmed *The Color Purple*, he called in Crouch to work on the score. When Disney produced *The Lion King*, Crouch produced much of the music. He wrote the title theme for the television show *Amen* and "Will You Be There" for the movie *Free Willy*; he even produced the music in *Handel's Messiah: A Soulful Celebration*. In his spare moments this legendary writer still found time to write a hundred new inspirational songs and pastor the Christ Memorial Church of God in Christ. He is living life as if there isn't a moment to waste, and, in truth, he believes there isn't!

For Andraé Crouch the spiritual journey that has opened the door to his success in gospel music started almost five decades ago. It was in his father's church that Crouch began singing for the Lord. Devoted to Christian service at an early age, after high school he took a job with an inner-city ministry trying to save and reform troubled juveniles. While working with teenage drug addicts, felons, and prostitutes, he sang and taught the gospel. For him, conversing with others about the power of the Holy Spirit has always been as natural as breathing.

"When I got out of high school," Crouch recalled, "I was working for the David Wilkerson Ministry. There was one guy in particular who was out of control. His attitude was always ugly. Larry was half white and half Mexican. How he hated the place. Yet he was kind of jazzy, so he really liked it when he heard me play and sing in chapel. As a matter of fact every time he wanted to leave, I would take him into the chapel and we would play and sing. He told me he couldn't get into the religious stuff we were teaching, but he liked my music."

Although it was tempting, Crouch didn't give up on Larry. Even when he had other important things to do, he often spent hours talking about problems with his charge. When Larry went ballistic, Crouch sang for him until he calmed down. When he was lonely, Crouch would be there for him too. Yet the weeks turned into months and all the words and prayers seemed to continually fall on deaf ears. Larry liked Crouch, but he didn't even believe God existed. It seemed that nothing the singer said could change the boy's mind. In a very real sense, Crouch wondered if he was just wasting his time. He questioned whether anything he was saying or doing would ever mean anything in the young man's life.

"I remember one chapel service," Crouch continued; "I was singing 'The Blood.' As I sang I looked around the chapel. Out of the corner of my eye I saw Larry weeping. When he saw me looking, he turned his head. He didn't want me to know the Lord was getting to him."

Not long after that chapel service, Larry gave himself to the Lord. He didn't do it in a mild manner either. He gripped religion in a vice-lock and became the loudest praiser in the program. He was as overpowering with his salvation as he has once been with his antireligious jargon.

"Man," Crouch laughed, "Larry became this 'Praise God' radical. I would take him with me when I sang in a church, and he was shouting Hallelujahs all the time. He was that excited by the power of God. When I left the program, Larry was still there and still praising the Lord!"

Immersed in recording and singing, Crouch's career grew to the point where he was rarely home. On the road for weeks at a time, he lost track of many of his old friends. Yet Larry managed to stay in touch. From time to time he would either seek out Crouch at a performance or call him at home.

"One day I got this phone call," Andraé recalled. "'Hey Andy,' it began. Andy is what Larry always called me. For a while we caught up, then he told me to read Luke 15. He was sure the message in the Scripture would move me to write the biggest song I had ever written. He guaranteed it. After I got off the phone I read it, but I didn't feel like anything had changed and went on about my day."

The next morning when Crouch got out of bed, he was moved to go to his piano. With the Scripture Larry had asked him to read weighing on his mind, he played a new song from beginning to end without even stopping to write down a word. It seemed as if God Himself was writing the work, as well as singing and playing it through him.

"I started crying," Crouch recalled. "Wow, it came through like that. It was incredible. I went to some friends' house for dinner that night, and I sang this song for them. They asked me where I had got the inspiration. I told them it was from Larry.

They laughed. They knew him too, and I think they had problems believing he could have been the source for the work."

Crouch titled the song "My Tribute" and immediately began to sing it in concert. Just as Larry had predicted, the response was like nothing Crouch had ever seen before. He couldn't wait to record "My Tribute" and send a copy to Larry. Yet before he could get to the studio, something happened.

"A month later," Crouch explained, "I received this phone call at four in the morning. An Oregon hospital was on the line. They explained that there was this guy who had been in a head-on wreck and the only name and number he gave them to contact was mine. He wanted me to pray for him."

At the instant Crouch got the call, Larry was in the I.C.U. with only a 40–60 chance of making it through the night. He had lost an eye, his heart had been bruised and his chest crushed. He was constantly fading in and out of consciousness.

"I asked the nurse who had called me," the singer related, "if there was any way I could talk to Larry. I told her I had to tell him something. She informed me she didn't know if there would be any response, but she'd try. She took the phone to his bed and I said, 'Larry, this Andy.' His voice was weak but he answered, 'I might not make it.' I told him, 'Yes you will. You know that song you wanted me to write? I wrote it.' I told him the words and said, 'This is for you,' and repeated the line, 'With His power He will raise you.'"

Crouch checked in with the hospital the next day and found that Larry had indeed improved. The nurses assured Crouch that while it would take some time, Larry was going to make it. After saying a prayer of thanks, the singer packed his bags and hit the road for another grueling round of concerts.

"About ten days later I was looking for a rest," Crouch recalled. "It was after a show, and there was a place I wanted to go to eat. For some reason we couldn't get there, so we went to this Dennys instead. From where I was sitting I couldn't see the entrance, but I suddenly heard this boisterous voice shouting 'Hallelujah!' I knew it had to be Larry, but I couldn't believe it. I knew he couldn't be well enough to be out of the hospital. I got up and sure enough it was Larry. He looked great! Even the scars had already been healed."

"My Tribute" began as a seed of friendship between a counselor and a wayward youth. It grew through a salvation experience and the Christian fellowship that followed. Now the song is in hundreds of hymnals and has been recorded more than three thousand times. Yet what makes Andraé Crouch happier than the success of "My Tribute" is that the once-troubled youth who inspired it is now the pastor of a growing church in California. To God be the glory for the great things He has done!

O Happy Day

$\mathcal{I}$t would seem to be a stretch for an Anglican pastor who was born in London, England, in 1702 to write a hit rock song for an African-American choir in 1969. Yet when the Lord's hand is at work, even those who have only Him in common often come together in very special ways and for very special reasons.

Philip Doddridge was fortunate to survive his youth. Of twenty children born to his mother, he was one of two to make it to adulthood. The son of a merchant, Philip was orphaned at thirteen. Because he was a brilliant student, academics saved him from a life on the streets. Given an opportunity for a free education at the Academy at Kibworth in Leicestershire, the youth not only became a scholar, he also accepted the Lord into his life. Moved by a need to serve, he entered the ministry in 1729. He continued to live his life for Christ until he died in Spain twenty-two years later.

A lover of words, Doddridge dabbled in poetry. One of his works was an attempt to define his emotions on the day he accepted Christ as his Savior. "O Happy Day That Fixed My Choice" was a joyous recounting of the peace and comfort God had brought into his formerly troubled life. Only four two-line stanzas long, the poem was Doddridge's testimony for the remainder of his life.

After his death the poem might have been lost if it had not been for a London publisher who published it as a hymn in 1755. Using an established musical score, the English pastor's testimony was then republished in many hymnals and found its way to the United States in the early 1800s.

In the States a chorus was added to the original verse, and the song was reset to music composed by noted songwriter Edward F. Rimbault. It is unknown if Rimbault knowingly contributed the music or if a third party borrowed the melody from one of the composer's earlier works. Nevertheless, this marriage of century-old British verses and new-world expression seemed perfect. Now complete with a refrain, "O Happy Day" quickly became a popular American hymn included in most of the Christian songbooks of the day. Sung millions of times, it remained unchanged for eleven decades.

More than two hundred years after Doddridge's testimony was first published, Edwin Hawkins became concerned that many of the youths he saw growing up in African-American churches had no real connection with their traditional gospel music roots. As the kids became more and more involved in the popular music of the sixties, they seemed to take less interest in the songs that had been an integral facet of black worship for years. Although he was classically trained, the Oakland, California, native had a keen sense of the importance of history. In order to keep alive the wonderful sounds from the past, Hawkins began to teach choir seminars steeped in gospel music. These clinics led to his forming the Northern State Youth Choir of California in 1967.

Hawkins' Youth Choir attacked traditional church songs with a vigor and freedom rarely shown by modern churches. Rather than having his group "sing it like it was written," the choirmaster gave them a chance to roll with the Spirit. Much like the spirituals of another era, Hawkins' kids allowed their imaginations to move them as they sang. What resulted were new takes on old songs. These reborn anthems jumped out of the dusty pages of songbooks and landed firmly in the joy that had traditionally defined black gospel music.

By 1969 composer and singer Paul Anka was so moved by the choir's performances that he helped secure an opportunity for the group to cut an album for Pavilion Records. In the studio Anka took over the role of producer, but he let the work of Hawkins and the kids stand as it was. He knew when not to tamper with something very special. What resulted was a collection of modern-day spirituals that represented gospel music in a way unheard by the masses for at least a generation.

The staff at Pavilion decided that the Edwin Hawkins Singers, as the group had now been renamed, had potential on the popular music charts. In a move unprecedented at the time, the label shipped a Christian single to rock radio outlets. Led by the strong solo work of Dorothy Combs Morrison, this release, "O Happy Day," soon found its way onto the charts, competing for playing time with songs such as The Beatles' "Get Back" and The 5th Dimension's "Aquarius/Let the Sunshine In." By May the gospel classic had flown past the top names of the rock era and landed in the top ten. "O Happy Day" would not back off the charts for nine more weeks.

There was great joy when Philip Doddridge came to know his Savior and "fixed his choice." The memory of that wonderful day moved him to write a poem fully defining his moment of grace. By a miracle Doddridge's words became a song that moved across an ocean and found its way into American church music. Then, just when it was being forgotten by most Christians, "O Happy Day" was brought back to life by a man who wanted to keep the joyous tradition of African-American gospel music alive. The song did more than honor the incredible passion of spiritual music, it also moved a nation in a way few gospel songs ever had.

Gospel music is the music of grace and joy. The words beg to be embraced by individuals who will place their own stamp of individuality on them. Gospel music isn't meant to sit on a page and be sung like a hymn, it is supposed to be set free like a bird to soar where the Spirit takes it. Philip Doddridge never heard true gospel music. Yet he knew the freedom and joy of salvation. How touched he probably would have been to know that the emotions he felt at the moment of grace were to live on with soaring wonder two centuries later in the voices of children who also knew the same Lord in the same way.

Peace in the Valley

Until the third decade of the twentieth century the term "gospel music" was unknown. Before that time every song written that embraced a religious theme was generally called either a hymn or a spiritual. In 1920, a decade before he became the most important figure in African-American religious music, Thomas A. Dorsey coined the term "gospel music" to describe a "hymn" he had written called "If You See My Savior." From this humble beginning it would take only a few years for the term "gospel" to be universally applied to almost all music using religious themes.

By the mid-thirties Dorsey had grown from a little-known songwriter and blues singer to the most important black composer of gospel music in the nation. Not only were his many original songs becoming the focal point of spiritual expression in the African-American community, but his work was finding wide acceptance in the largely white world of southern gospel as well.

Dorsey's decade-long charge to the top of the religious music market in both white and black circles was due in part to his presence in the fabulously successful African-American music conferences and evangelical conventions of the era, coupled with the fact that the giants in the southern gospel publishing industry began to use his songs in their widely distributed hymnbooks. First at the Stamps-Baxter company in Dallas, then at R.E. Winsett and Homer Rodeheaver's publishing houses, Dorsey's words and music crossed racial boundaries and opened the doors of many white churches for the composer's special type of musical odes influenced by black blues. Thus, even while Dorsey was bringing a new kind of religious substance and zeal to his own people, he was also influencing hundreds of white composers and performers. The effects of this influence did more than change the feel of white religious music, it also sharply influenced country, rockabilly, and rock and roll, too. Such was the impact of Dorsey's blending various musical styles.

The movement of musical ideas and influences was not a one-way street limited to those who listened to the composer's work. By the late thirties Dorsey himself was involved in a growth period in which he observed the current strains of the hillbilly music of the South and also studied the spiritual and religious themes from the past. One of the songs he latched onto and that stuck in his mind was "We Shall Walk Through the Valley of Peace."

"Walk Through the Valley" had originally been a Negro-slave spiritual developed and sung during the long days working in the cotton fields. Dorsey must have been deeply affected by the vision of men and women who were being held captive and forced to labor for an all-powerful master and still in the midst of their suffering were somehow able to dwell on the hope for peace and security that was just out of their reach. They were looking to a better time when they would be rewarded for their hard work and suffering.

After months of thought the image of the composer's own slave ancestors' trials and tribulations seemed to come into sharp focus during a train ride in 1939. As his Pullman car raced past the pastoral scenes of an Indiana countryside, the composer turned again to "Walk Through the Valley of Peace" for inspiration.

At the very time of his trip, Dorsey and all of America were being bombarded with the news of Hitler's war machine racing through Eastern Europe and enslaving a new generation of captives. The peace that reigned supreme in the Indiana countryside was an unimaginable dream for millions.

"It was just before Hitler sent his war chariots into Western Europe," the composer would later tell others, that he received his inspiration for "Peace in the Valley." "I was on a train going through southern Indiana on the way to Cincinnati, and the country seemed to be upset about this coming war that he [Hitler] was about to bring on. I passed through a valley on the train. Horses, cows, and sheep were all grazing together in this little valley. A little brook was running through the valley, and up the hill there I could see where the water was falling from. Everything seemed so peaceful with all the animals down there grazing together. It made me wonder what's the matter with humanity? What's the matter with mankind? Why couldn't man live in peace like the animals down there?"

Dorsey was so troubled by these questions that he took pen and paper and began to scribble down what was on his heart. Influenced heavily by the field spiritual he had been humming for months, his new song quickly took shape, except now the old spiritual had been given a plaintive quality that did not so much take on the character of the blues as the hillbilly feel of southern white music. For the composer this song seemed like a radical departure from his normal writing style, yet it would prove to be as inspired as the lyrics themselves. Dorsey's simple plea for peace would give birth to a work that would come to touch millions.

It should come as no surprise that "Peace in the Valley" became an important part of the gospel music world during the height of World War II. Yet, though it was recorded and performed by scores of artists during this period and became an integral facet of African-American and small southern rural white congregational singing, the song would not become uni-versally accepted and treasured until a hillbilly performer began to use it as a part of both his radio show and concerts.

Clyde Julian "Red" Foley had been singing professionally since his teens. Born in Kentucky in 1910, Red migrated to Chicago during the Depression. He landed a job there as a reg-ular on WLS's popular *National Barn Dance* radio show. By the war years he had become one of the most popular hillbilly per-formers and record sellers in the nation.

Foley had grown up with a special love for southern church music and then, when he had first moved to Chicago, had been heavily influenced by black blues. With this unique musical per-spective, it should come as little surprise that when Foley first heard Thomas A. Dorsey's "Peace in the Valley," the singer thought he had found a song that not only embraced all the major musical influences of his life—gospel, blues, and country—but also gave him the perfect message for a world in conflict.

Using a standard southern gospel arrangement coupled with a country music backup group, Foley placed the Dorsey classic on the country music charts in 1951. With the Sunshine Boys quartet providing the backup, his single was certified gold and became one of the most loved "country" songs in the nation. The song helped pave the singer's way into the Coun-try Music Hall of Fame and was so much associated with Foley that there is still a mistaken impression that he actually wrote "Peace in the Valley."

One of the those who was mesmerized by Foley's recording of the gospel song was young Elvis Presley. Elvis was a boy who had cut his teeth on the all-night "singin's," which were an important part of the rural South in the thirties and forties. Gospel music was Presley's first love. He even auditioned for a spot in the famous Blackwood Quartet just months before he landed his own recording contract and changed the course of popular music.

While Foley had taken "Peace in the Valley" to millions of country music fans, it was Presley who introduced the song to the world. During one of his highly publicized guest shots on the *Ed Sullivan Show* in 1956, Elvis and the Jordanaires Quartet, using a Foley-type arrangement, performed the Thomas A. Dorsey composition for a national television audience. The song literally changed the public's perception of the singer from that of rebel to "All-American" boy. The response to Elvis's live rendition of the gospel song was so great that an extended play 45 RPM record was quickly cut and shipped to outlets. This "EP," anchored by "Peace in the Valley," became the largest-selling record of its type in music history.

Through Red Foley and Elvis Presley "Peace in the Valley" became one of the ten best-known gospel standards of all time. By the early sixties almost every major white and black religious artist had cut what would become the very best known of all the Dorsey classics. Its legend grew even larger in 1968 when Red Foley closed a Fort Wayne, Indiana, concert with the song and then died of a heart attack. To all those who knew the performer it seemed fitting that he closed his life with a song that had meant so much to his career and his faith.

In 1993, at the age of ninety-three, Dorsey himself made his trip to the valley that offered the promise of eternal peace. Yet the former blues singer who invented the term "gospel music" left behind such a strong legacy of musical works that his influence will no doubt continue to touch, inspire, and comfort millions for generations to come. That is why he is still called the Father of Gospel Music, a title he no doubt deserves.

Precious Lord, Take My Hand

*B*orn in 1899, Thomas A. Dorsey, the man who would become known as the Father of Gospel Music, was the son of a traveling preacher. Raised in Atlanta, Dorsey early on recognized that opportunities for blacks in the South of that time were few. So it was not surprising that while still in his teens he drifted to Chicago to ply his trade as a musician. Far from the church pews and hymnals of his youth, he went astray as he earned his living playing his "whispering" piano in bars and brothels on the city's south side.

Dorsey was ambitious and recognized that playing the piano in seedy night spots was never going to give him much of a chance for professional advancement. In 1920 he took his earnings and entered the Chicago School of Composition. His studies quickly paid off. Late in the year he wrote and sold what became a minor blues hit, "If You Don't Believe I'm Leaving, You Can Count the Days I'm Gone."

However, illness prevented him from cashing in on his first attempt at fame. Thin, worn, and racked with pain, he dropped out of school, was hospitalized for weeks, and almost gave up on life altogether. Then on September 21, 1921, just at the time he hit bottom, an uncle took him to hear the singing and preaching at the all-black National Baptist Convention. Dorsey was so moved by W.M. Nix's rendition of "I Do, Don't You?" that he surrendered his life to writing gospel music's good news. Joining the choir at the New Hope Baptist Church, he set himself to composing religious music that had the feel and spirit of the blues. The problem was that no one would sing or publish it. Within a year Dorsey was back playing the blues on the night-club circuit.

With compositions such as "I Just Want a Daddy I Can Call My Own" and "Muddy Water Blues," Dorsey quickly became a mildly popular composer of what was then called "race" music. Over the next few years his status grew, and by the mid-twenties top blues artists such as Ma Rainey were cutting his songs. Dorsey would probably even have established himself as a successful solo club act if he had not become ill again in 1926. Dorsey considered suicide and later said that he would have surely died if Bishop H.H. Haley hadn't stepped in and brought the Lord back into his life. Bishop Haley reintroduced Dorsey to living a daily life of faith, and this caused him to turn again to writing only Christian songs. Yet when he was still greeted with no success selling his "gospel" music, he returned to more commercial outlets.

Now married and in need of a way to provide for a family, Dorsey teamed with a blues singer named Tampa Red to write "It's Tight Like That." The song bordered on being too crude to record, but that didn't stop it from becoming a hit in the local blues market. More important for Dorsey than the song's radio and juke-box play, the number generated several thousand dollars in royalties. These funds finally gave him the freedom to devote himself full time to religious music.

In 1931 Dorsey became the director of music at Chicago's Ebenezer Baptist Church. His third try at giving his life to Christian music was successful, as he quickly rose to an elite status in black-church music circles of the time. Within a year his new kind of religious music was so popular that several times a month he was on the road performing for church conventions. After each performance Dorsey sold stacks of sheet music to choir directors and parishioners who could hardly wait to race back to their home churches with these new gospel sounds.

In 1932 Dorsey, now fully committed to using his music to spread the gospel, was asked to go to St. Louis to lead a large revival meeting and premier his latest compositions. Normally he would have jumped at this opportunity, but this time he hesitated. Hettie, his wife, was nine months pregnant, and he didn't want to leave her with the time for delivery so close. Once, even while heading to the meeting, he turned back. Yet after returning home and checking on his sleeping wife, he got back into his car and made the trip.

The first night in St. Louis went well. Yet those who knew Dorsey noted that he seemed to be consumed by an unexplained sense of pain and worry. On the second day of the revival, he was paged. There was a telegram from Chicago. When he opened it, he learned that he was the father of a baby boy but that Hettie had died in childbirth. Dorsey rushed back to Chicago. Even as he mourned his wife, he held his new son in his arms, thanking God he had something of his beloved wife to treasure. Yet the following day the child also died, seemingly robbing him of everything that had been his dear Hettie.

Dorsey was heartbroken. For the next week he slept little and ate even less. He couldn't begin to fathom a life without his family. Nor could he make any sense of why this had happened. For hours on end he blamed God for cursing him with this burden of sorrow. He thought of walking away from his faith, his profession, and his music.

After the funeral a still disconsolate Dorsey returned to his piano in an attempt to use music to ease his grief. The blues, the style that had first brought him a measure of fame, the music that had taken him into bars and speakeasies, now called out to him to express his pain. And yet even as he wallowed in self-pity and yearned to escape anything that had to do with his present life, another voice seemed to call out to him too. And as he ran his hands over the keys, that second voice wouldn't leave him alone. Taking up a pen, the thirty-three-year-old composer quickly scribbled down the lyrics to a song that came to him as easily as a gentle spring rain. Sitting alone and putting a bluesy melody line to the words, he quietly and sincerely sang a prayer that was not only to become one of his most beloved musical contributions but also to serve to rejoin the composer's own tie to his Lord.

Seeking out his friend Theodore Fry, Dorsey shared "Take My Hand, Blessed Lord" with the preacher. Fry, moved deeply by the song's message, suggested only that he change "Blessed Lord" to "Precious Lord." After much prayer, he did.

When given the opportunity, the Lord can positively use any experience, even those gained in bars and brothels. Without his background in blues and their message of pain it is doubtful that Dorsey could ever have composed "Take My Hand, Precious Lord." Yet the fact that he was able to combine his suffering and his musical experience into a song that would be recorded hundreds of times by artists of all colors and faiths and translated into thirty-two languages didn't ever mean as much to Thomas Dorsey as having that song build a bridge between him and his Lord. In 1932, when Jesus took Dorsey's hand, the composer gave the world a prayer that reminds us all that the Lord's hand is still there for each of us.

Satisfied

$\mathcal{B}$y 1950 Martha Carson was almost thirty years old and with her husband, James, had put together a successful country duet team called the Barn Dance Sweethearts. Known for their solid country harmonies on classic gospel sounds, the Carsons were Knoxville's WNOX's biggest stars. Then, just when Nashville and the *Opry* began to take an interest in the duo, James divorced his wife of nine years.

Martha was crushed. She told her friends that James's move had broken her heart. Unprepared for a life alone, it was only the grace of God, the goodwill of friends, and the loyalty of the management of WNOX that got Carson through the months after the very public break-up. Yet, even as she played her guitar and sang her songs, the fall-out from her divorce continued to follow the beautiful young woman everywhere she went. In the South of the early fifties divorce was considered almost unforgivable by many.

WNOX began to get mail from listeners demanding to know why they would allow a divorced woman to sing religious music on the air. It was almost as if Carson had a red *A* painted across her chest. She became a target for many who claimed faith in God but who seemed to have no forgiveness in their hearts. With each letter, with each cruel word, Martha's already shattered confidence sank even lower. How she wanted to explain that the divorce was not her idea. How she wanted to share with her fans just what she had been through before James had left. But her faith demanded she remain silent and allow people to form their own ideas about her life and her behavior based on what others were saying.

What only Martha and her close friends knew was that long before he divorced her, James had committed adultery with numerous women, spent many nights drunk and verbally abusive, and, even though he still sang gospel songs on the air and at live shows, had denied any belief in God at all. Although she had been given every possible reason in the eyes of God and man to dissolve her union, Martha had forgiven her husband time and time again, praying for him each night he was away from her, and begging him each Sunday to come back to church with her. Now, constantly belittled, she silently faced the slings and arrows of a public that seemed to side with James.

As with so many who have been falsely judged, Martha turned her eyes back to God not only to seek answers but to find peace. Yet even through Bible study, prayer, and the support of Christian friends, her faith did not strengthen. As she worked before live audiences, she became a frightened, lonely child, wondering how each man and woman was judging her.

One night she was waiting in a car with singer and show host Bill Carlisle when, just minutes away from show time, she completely broke down. She couldn't stop crying, and the last thing she wanted to do was walk onto a stage just to be a target for more abuse. Nothing anyone said to her mattered. In her mind she wasn't going on that night or ever again. All she wanted to do was run away and hide from world.

Martha later said that as she sobbed she felt the Lord telling her, "Don't worry. I'm satisfied and you're satisfied." The words eased her tears. Now alone in the car, for the first time in weeks she felt a bit of hope. Looking around, she found a blank check on the floor of the car and retrieved a pen from her purse. Scribbling as fast as she could, words gushing from her soul more than her mind, on the back of that blank check Martha jotted down a set of lyrics that would symbolize her acceptance of things she couldn't change, as well as the strength she could draw from Christ in even the darkest times.

"Satisfied" became her theme song and signaled a dramatic departure from the slow, country-style gospel songs she had been performing. When she picked up her guitar and added music to her heartfelt words, "Satisfied" rocked—long before that term was invented. Rapidly paced, using a speeded-up segment of "That Old-Time Religion" as a beginning and ending, Carson's "Satisfied" was very different from other gospel songs attempted by most solo performers. There was an energy and life to her composition that not only had people jumping and clapping their hands but paying attention to the message, too.

After hearing it just once, Chet Atkins sensed that "Satisfied" could become a hit record. But as Martha would soon discover, thanks to a contract she had signed with Capitol Records, it didn't seem it could be one for her. Capitol considered her a duet act. If she was going to record for them, she would have to find a partner to replace her ex-husband. While Martha didn't mind singing duets, she wanted to be able to cut her personal testimony by herself. Finally, in late 1951, Capitol gave in, tore up her old contract, and signed her as a solo act.

Her first single was "Satisfied." She followed this country-gospel hit with "Journey to the Sky," "Let the Light Shine on Me," "This Ole House," and "Swing Down, Chariot." At gospel and country shows, her enthusiastic and highly charged performances not only brought the audience to its feet but also caused other performers to come out of their dressing rooms and watch her from the wings. By the mid-fifties, the now RCA artist was influencing many of the nation's top gospel acts as well as country and pop performers. Faron Young, Ferlin

Huskey, and even Elvis Presley slipped into Martha's shows and cornered her for advice.

Martha Carson went on to enjoy a long career, singing mostly gospel music. Her "Satisfied" was recorded and performed hundreds of times by scores of artists from every music genre. And yet in a very real sense, no matter if it was sung by a gospel quartet or a solo artist, performed at a concert or in a church, "Satisfied" served as a road map of faith for those who have seen the world crash down around them. It therefore seems appropriate that when the Lord inspired her to write the song that would not only lift her spirits but also jump-start her career, she wrote those words on a blank check. A blank check is exactly what Christ has offered everyone who will come to the Cross and believe in Him, and that is why Martha and millions of others are "Satisfied."

Stand by Me

Charles Tindley was a big man. Barrel-chested, with a chis-eled body, the six-foot-four African-American preacher weighed over two hundred pounds. In the late 1800s and early 1900s Tindley was an imposing figure behind the pulpit and on the street.

From 1885 to 1902, Tindley pastored several churches up and down the Eastern seaboard. Known as much for his singing as for his outstanding preaching, he was eventually called to Philadelphia to pastor the church where he had once worked as a janitor. During his three decades of leadership, the John Wes-ley Methodist Church changed its name to East Calvary Methodist, built a sanctuary that seated more than three thou-sand, and grew to claim ten thousand active members. This incredible growth was, by the grace of God, due largely to the charisma, strength, vision, and leadership of Charles Tindley.

At a time when most black Americans tried to keep a low profile, Tindley stood tall. He united the African-American community in Philadelphia not only with his strong preaching but also through his daily life. Taking his ministry beyond the walls of his church, he began organizations that helped poor people save money, find jobs, get home loans, and obtain edu-cation. He organized food and clothing drives, found shelter for homeless people, and even built a soup kitchen in his church's basement.

Strolling the street each day, he sought out beggars and gave them both food and spiritual guidance. He walked into bars and bordellos and witnessed without judging. He knocked on the doors of homes, businesses, and schools, encouraging everyone he met to take the high road, to give as they had received, and always to look for a soul who needed a friend.

Maybe it was because of his activism and the way he carried himself that this son of a slave was unique. He transcended race at a time when nothing and no one else did. Often over half of those who gathered to hear him preach on Sunday were white. Prominent white seminaries of the day even sent their students to hear Dr. Tindley's sermons.

Charles Tindley didn't just rely on his messages, he also used music to draw people to the Lord. His services were peppered with gospel, classical, and spiritual songs. He used them to set moods and to set up his sermons. By the time he arrived at his Philadelphia pastorate, he had composed a dozen gospel songs, and he used them to emphasize the important points of his most famous sermons.

Tindley had overcome much to rise to power. He had known the bonds of slavery, oppression, and poverty. Yet he had not been held back. He had refused to give in. Still, he was acutely aware that the hard life facing most blacks at this time gave them little hope, comfort, or joy. Most of the people in his congregation felt trapped. They knew they would never have riches or be given equal rights. Not as strong as Tindley, most African-Americans of this era had grown to accept the fact that they were viewed as second-class citizens, and because of this their spirits had been partly broken.

Charles Tindley used his messages and songs to show that God had a reason for making his congregation go through such great trials. He preached that those who walked bravely through the fires of this life would become purified like gold ore being melted in a furnace. Yet being pure and faithful wasn't enough for Tindley. He felt that Christians, even those who were being oppressed by the world, should also reach out to others and lift them up.

One of his favorite sermon illustrations concerned a peach tree: "You've never seen a peach tree eat its own peaches," he used to say. "But you have seen a tree so laden with fruit that its branches reached the ground so a toddler can pick and partake. Our lives should be like that tree. Not what we maintain for ourselves, but give to others, as God gave His Son. I want to be like that tree, serve others, share what I can with others."

Often when Tindley preached of the peach tree, he would use his own rich voice to sing "Stand by Me." In this slow, moving song, Tindley not only wrote of the tests and trials he and his members faced each day, but he also presented the vision of God standing by them in these times. Through their rich fabric, the lyrics also sent forth a challenge to Christians to stand by others who were in need.

In each stanza of "Stand by Me" Tindley eloquently and simply voiced the hurdles faced by his congregation. He sang of tribulations, faults and failures, persecution and weakness. The crowning point of the song was the fact that the preacher not only believed that God would always be there to stand by him, but as a representative of the Lord he would be there to help others in need as well. As he sang "Stand by Me," he brought hope to his people and also helped them to fully comprehend just how important it was for them to seek out the lost, feed the hungry, clothe the naked, and reach out to those living in sin. Thus "Stand by Me" became a living testimony of a man who used every opportunity to reach out for Jesus.

The story of the great preacher Charles Tindley has now largely been forgotten. His works of charity and outreach have been lost in time, and though the church where he preached now bears his name, few outside that church even know who he is. Yet the songs that he wrote to explain God's message have not been lost. "Stand by Me" has been recorded countless times and was even rewritten into a rock-and-roll standard. Other songs of Tindley have had their influence too. "I Shall Overcome" was turned into an anthem for the civil-rights movement, and "When the Morning Comes" has become a favorite hymn in tens of thousands of churches.

Tindley was born a slave, but he died a free man. It wasn't just Lincoln who freed him, it was also Jesus. Lincoln couldn't stand by him for long, for he died. Yet Jesus was there always for him, and even in the storms of life Charles Tindley's lasting faith and words assure us that He is still standing by us today.

Supper Time

*B*y the mid-forties Ira Stanphill had become one of the most noted songwriters and evangelists in the nation. His sheet music and songbooks were sold in every state, he was invited to sing and minister from coast to coast, and was often teamed with the best-known preachers America had to offer. He had come a long way from his days as the son of a Kansas telegraph operator. Yet, as he tightly clutched a folded piece of paper and watched his small son Butch sleep in a bed in the corner of a dingy hotel room, he wished he could go back home to a simpler and more stable time.

The United States was at war on two fronts, and those who turned out to hear Ira sing were looking to him for hope and inspiration. Yet the lack of security created by the times coupled with his call to evangelize for a time in Los Angeles had taken a toll on him as well. Ira had married a beautiful and talented young woman who had joined him in his ministry. During the days before World War II the couple had even written "Room at the Cross," one of the most endearing invitational hymns ever composed. While on the surface the Stanphills seemed to have a marriage as perfect as the harmonies of their duets, behind closed doors a battle of epic proportions was constantly brewing.

When Ira traveled, his wife, Zelma, grew bored. Her boredom grew into a series of affairs with servicemen. Although her husband had forgiven her several times and the couple had tried to start anew more than once, it seemed that she could fight off temptations for only a few months at a time. Not long after the birth of their son, Butch, she again began a sordid relationship with a soldier she had met at a religious meeting.

Feeling that Los Angeles offered nothing but temptation for his wife, Ira decided a change of pace might save the marriage. Giving up a solid job and a nice home, he moved his family across the country. For a while things improved, but then Zelma resumed her old ways. Finally, in a last-ditch effort to put their union on solid ground, the Stanphills moved back to the city where they had met—Springfield, Missouri.

Zelma stayed behind, but sent Butch with Ira, when the evangelist ministered in several summer revivals. At one of the stops, a surprised Stanphill was served with divorce papers. His zest for writing gone, a sense of great failure engulfing not only his personal life but also his ministry, Ira found himself questioning his worth as a songwriter, preacher, and father. As he watched his tiny son sleep, depression darkened his mood even more.

Ira had grown up in a loving family. He had gained tremendous strength from the security and love given him by his parents. Their witness and lifestyle had been the reason he had first felt God's touch in his life. There was little doubt it was his father and mother who had guided him to a point where he was ready to accept a full-time call to work in Christian service. For years he had prayed he could give his own children this same kind of home, faith, and security he had known as a child. Now as his wife sought to sever a commitment that Ira had thought would last until the death of one of them, he realized his son would never know the kind of home life he himself had so treasured.

In an effort to escape the sense of guilt that now clouded his judgment and caused him to question his own worth, Ira let his thoughts carry him back to his childhood. The image that came quickly into focus was of him and his brother playing in a friend's yard just before sunset. In the midst of recalling that childhood adventure, he heard his mother's voice calling out to them from down the block, "Ira, Ray, come home, it's supper time."

Taking pen in hand, Stanphill expanded on his vision. Within just a few moments "Supper Time" became more than just a call for a boy to come and eat; it became a Christian testimony for those nearing death. It also grew into Ira's most popular and most recorded composition.

At the moment he wrote "Supper Time," Ira couldn't see how his own son would ever relate to the song's words. He knew that he and Zelma would never get back together. He was also committed as a Christian to hold his marriage vows to his ex-wife intact. As long as she lived, he didn't feel that he should marry again. So, even as he completed one of his most poetic and beautiful songs, a testimony that would come to touch millions, he bowed his head and cried. He knew that while he could provide the words, he could not figure out a way to make his inspiration a reality for his own son.

In that dingy hotel room Ira prayed for guidance as a parent. He also prayed that in spite of this tragic situation, Butch would somehow come to know the love and security that only a Christian family could bring. Yet even as he later held his son in his arms and told him how much he loved him, he doubted that there could be an answer to this prayer.

Five years later another unexpected tragedy hit Stanphill. Zelma was killed in an automobile accident. Her death created a void in Butch's life that Ira attempted to fill. Yet try as he would, he could never be both mother and father to his child.

In the Lord's good providence, not long after Zelma's passing, Ira married a young woman who not only became his wife and partner in work but also embraced Butch as her own son. For a man who had once seen no way to ever be a part of a Christian family again, a woman named Gloria gave him more than he had ever dreamed.

One evening Ira was watching his new bride fix the evening meal. Everything in the kitchen smelled so good he could hardly wait to sit down at the table. As she set the final dish on the table, Ira shook his head in wonder and thought of what a glorious wife he had been given. Failing to notice her husband's obvious admiration, Gloria looked around for a moment, then walked to the back door. Strolling out onto the porch, the sunset framing her face, she called out, "Butch, come home, it's supper time."

Although Gloria might not have noticed, a smile brightened Ira Stanphill's face and tears welled up in his eyes. The Lord had not only given him a song that touched millions but had answered a parent's earnest prayer as well.

The Sweetest Song I Know

The greatest writer of gospel music was born in the Indian Territory (now Oklahoma) on October 29, 1905. The son of a dirt-poor cotton farmer, Albert Edward Brumley was to gospel music what Hank Williams Sr. was to country music. They were both masters of taking the unadorned facets of life, painting them in simple words, and framing the finished product in an unforgettable melody. Artists without brushes, historians of singular moments, men who understood the needs of others, Brumley and Williams had a genius that burst forth in songs that everyone could sing and that millions adopted as their own. The obvious difference between these two song scribes was that one toiled in darkness, whereas the other worked in the light.

It was the light that pushed Brumley to write. He understood that people needed the light and that their attitudes were better when they could see it. Therefore many of the more than eight hundred songs that sprang from his lifetime of experience touched upon potentially tragic situations where pain and suffering were eased by hope and faith.

In 1941 the world was indeed fighting in the darkness. World War II was beckoning the United States and its people. While millions were praying and hoping a miracle would stop the bloodshed before it reached our shores, as the reports from Europe and China came back day after day and the enemies of a free world made greater gains against the countries we called our allies, it seemed that the United States was indeed headed for front-line fighting. In the midst of the uncertainties of the time, Albert Brumley was inspired to write on a theme that had once inspired a struggling seaman. Basing a new gospel concept around "Amazing Grace," he gave birth to a song for the uncertainties of 1941 and of all the years to follow.

Brumley had an incredible ability for using words to paint a picture in words. In a sense he was an artist whose canvas was paper and whose ink spelled rather than drew. Yet when he finished each of his works of art, there were no abstract strokes. His final product represented real life presented in a very real way. Even a child could look at Brumley's musical paintings and understand what was behind each of them. Yet, though elementary in form, there was a very powerful message in his songs and perhaps especially in "The Sweetest Song I Know."

"It took me a long time to understand that he was more than just a dad," Albert Jr. recalled. "I was older before I began to understand how smart he was and how much he understood people's thoughts and feelings. Yet that is why his songs touched so many people. He knew what they needed.

"Dad used to say that people write songs all the time, but the only ones that audiences remember are the songs they can sing after hearing them just one or two times. So even as he wrote about the most complex spiritual matters, he always tried to keep his message simple."

When Brumley sat down to compose "The Sweetest Song I Know," he must have been aware of how many lost men were soon going to be locked in life-and-death combat. The thoughts of sinners losing their lives for their countries before giving their lives to the Lord must have troubled him greatly. His sincere prayer was for everyone to find eternal grace before they met death face to face. In order for him to bring forth this testimony, he turned to his own life for inspiration.

For the hook line in "The Sweetest Song I Know," Brumley had to search no further than one of the most beloved hymns ever written. It was a song he had heard his mother sing many times as she worked. Using the positive outlook that was so much a part of his life, he built on the most familiar line of "Amazing Grace" and shaped it to fit his new, uplifting composition.

When Brumley finished it, "The Sweetest Song I Know" was both a trip back to the past and a wonderful look to the future. In a very magical way, he had taken the memories of growing up with "Amazing Grace" and included scenes of home, family, and church. In just a few simple verses he had praised Christian mothers, church services, choral anthems, and gospel singings. Through his text, he presented several references not only to "Amazing Grace" but also to several other well-known hymns. By the final stanza, his song had transported each listener back to his or her youth and had given them a renewed love of family and a sense of belonging, while also touching upon many of the classics that made up the "Christian hit parade."

"When Dad talked about writing," his son remembered, "he always talked about how important it was for the masses to understand him. In his viewpoint that was the key to bringing a song to life. It had to have something that grabs and holds people's attention."

With all its references to familiar facets of a Christian family, "The Sweetest Song I Know" grabbed people's attention in a hurry. And because this new song wasn't just a rehash of an old one but was a happy, joyful reminder of both the homes of the past and a heavenly home just around the bend, it kept folks singing, too. This was the kind of song that a nation going to war needed. Soldiers could sing it and feel their mother's touch and their home church's love. Mothers could sing it as a prayer for their own sons a world away. Fathers, brothers, sisters, and wives could relate to and cling to the lyrics for strength. In just a few simple words, Brumley had given everyone something to hold onto.

As masterful as "The Sweetest Song I Know" was, it might have been forgotten if not for the Happy Goodmans. That singing family related so much to this song because they had grown up in a family like the one Brumley described. The uptempo beat and four-part harmony were perfect for their blend. It was also the happiest song the Happy Goodmans knew. And it made everyone who heard it happy too.

Albert Brumley's optimism, his devotion to God and family, and his love of Christian service live on through each of his songs. Yet if any song he wrote is truly autobiographical and fully represents his positive personality, it has to be "The Sweetest Song I Know." It is truly amazing that he could put so many memories and ideas and so much inspiration in such a short message, but "amazing" quite accurately describes the work of this man who knew firsthand the joy of grace.

Thanks to Calvary

*M*ost writers are inspired by certain situations and experiences. If they had taken a different path in life, if fate had fallen differently, then they would never have met many of the people and never experienced many of the events that moved them to create. As Christians, Bill and Gloria Gaither strongly believe that fate had nothing to do with their meeting while one was teaching and the other substituting at a small Indiana high school. It was God who brought them together not only to fall in love and become husband and wife but also to join their talents in a mighty Christian mission.

In the mid-sixties Bill was teaching high school English and also leading the music program at a church in Anderson. Among those who attended the services and enjoyed Bill and Gloria's frequent specials was Doug Oldham.

Oldham was a familiar figure in the Midwest. A large man with a booming voice, he was the son of one of the area's most beloved ministers. With a background in Christian music and evangelism, Doug appeared to be the perfect father, husband, and witness. Yet, out of the public eye, Oldham's life was falling apart. For reasons he didn't understand, he was often consumed with rage. Anything could set him off. His wife and children were often the targets of his abuse. Love had been replaced by fear in his house, and Doug often saw hate in the eyes of the very ones who used to love him. No one, not even the closest of his friends, would have believed the real situation in the family's home life. It had become hell on earth.

When she could take no more, when she had come to the point where she feared for her own safety and was worried the children would be scarred so deeply their spirits would never heal, Laura Oldham gave up and admitted defeat. When she left Doug, taking their children with her, he hit rock bottom. Constantly alone, bitterness haunting his every waking hour, Doug fell into a thousand pieces. Awash in self-pity and sadness, he became so embittered with the hand "fate" had dealt him that he loaded a gun and placed the muzzle to his head. Yet try as he might, he couldn't find the courage to pull the trigger. Crying, hopeless and distraught, he fell to his knees and prayed for God to take his life. When his prayer wasn't answered, he questioned why a man who had sunk so low should be forced to live in the mess he had made of his life.

It was only after failing to follow through on his suicide attempt that Doug turned to the Bible and Christian friends. It was really the only course left for one who didn't have the courage to end his life. Through months of study, prayer, and heart-to-heart talks, he not only found a reason to live, but he also escaped the frustrations and demons that had caused him to lash out at those who were closest to him. When he regained his faith and his self-respect, he opened the lines of communication with his wife. Admitting all his mistakes, begging for forgiveness and another opportunity to be a responsible husband and father, Oldham finally convinced Laura they had something worth saving. Yet the trust his wife placed in him as she gave him another chance did not come as easy for his children. They had endured his madness when he had been with them and joy when he had been away. They didn't want to go back to the world that had brought them so much pain.

Doug's three daughters were scared of their father. Everything about their past life with him gave them nightmares. In an attempt to restore the children's confidence and trust, Doug and Laura sold their old home and moved to a new house where there were no bad memories. Yet even as they packed up the stuff in the old home, when the girls would see their father, they would often run and hide. After having his heart and spirit broken several times by the sight of his children fleeing from him, Doug finally decided to try to put into words the miracle of change that had happened in his heart. Finding a trembling daughter hiding behind a door in their old home, Doug gently hugged the frightened child and whispered, "Don't worry, you don't have to be afraid. We're moving to a new life. Thanks to Calvary, we don't live here anymore."

A few days after they had moved, Laura told Gloria Gaither the story of Doug's bonding confession to his daughter. Borrowing his testimonial line, "Thanks to Calvary," Gloria composed lyrics that told not only the story of Doug's fall from grace and journey back to a Christian walk but also the story of any person who had wandered in sin and had come back to the Cross to ask for and experience life-changing forgiveness.

As his life had inspired the lyrics, it seemed appropriate that Doug Oldham was the first performer to sing "Thanks to Calvary." It became both his signature song and his testimony. Thanks in large part to Gloria Gaither's pen, Doug was able to share secrets about his life in a way that would help others overcome guilt, frustration, and fear in their own worlds.

"Thanks to Calvary" has become one of the most recorded modern gospel music songs. Simple in both message and music, it has become more than just another biographical piece. In Gloria's words and Doug's life there is a profound truth that can be realized by any man, woman, or child. No matter where you have been, what you have done, or how badly you have sinned, thanks to what happened on a cross at Calvary, you can start fresh again.

This Ole House

Of all the hundreds of thousands of men and women from around the world who made decisions for Christ at Billy Graham crusades, Stuart Hamblen probably brought with him the highest profile. Singer, songwriter, actor, radio-show host, and one of Hollywood's best-known people, when Stuart walked the aisle inside a canvas tent in 1949, his life changed as few others ever had. Overcome by zeal, totally consumed by the Spirit, Hamblen left the revival that night reborn and regenerated with an incredible desire to tell others the good news of salvation.

A co-star in many of John Wayne's, Roy Rogers', and Gene Autry's movies, Hamblen first gave his new faith a voice through a radio show, *Cowboy Church of the Air.* Broadcast on Sunday morning, this show not only featured the testimonies of many important show-business personalities, but it was also a forum for Hamblen to premier some of the country/gospel songs he had written since being saved. Those tuning in each week were usually the first to hear such originals as "Open Up Your Heart and Let the Sun Shine In," "The Lord Is Counting on You," "You Must Be Born Again," "Until Then," "Your First Day in Heaven," and "It Is No Secret." When listeners heard the songs, they were almost always treated to Hamblen's telling why he had been inspired to write them. Over time he discovered that the combination of the song and the story helped many listeners seek Christ's will for their own lives.

Even after he was saved and stopped partying, Stuart remained popular with many Hollywood insiders. They loved his stories and were entranced by his energetic personality and inspired by his enthusiasm for life. Many of his cowboy friends, such as John Wayne, also respected his honesty and his love of wide-open spaces.

This is probably the reason John Wayne often accompanied him when he went on hunting trips. These outings sometimes lasted weeks and were punctuated by long hikes to remote areas and nights spent talking of matters of the heart by campfire. For Hamblen the game the friends brought back was not nearly as important as getting away to study firsthand the magnificence of God's natural handiwork. Because of the demands made on him for performances, speaking engagements, and other obligations, which had been increased by his very public faith, the times away from phones and audiences were moments of renewal.

On one of these getaway trips deep into the mountains, Hamblen noted in the distance a solitary cabin almost hidden among the trees. Curious as to the kind of man who would live so far from civilization, he urged his friends to follow him up the side of a mountain to the tiny shack. As they drew closer and noted there was no smoke coming from the stone chimney, the men began to believe that the place had been deserted and that their long climb would offer little more than a place to rest for a few moments before they made their way back down to their camp.

As they approached the cabin, Stuart hollered out a greeting. He didn't hear a human reply, but he smiled as he heard a dog barking behind the closed front door. *Maybe*, he thought, *there is someone here.*

As the hunting party stepped onto the porch, they heard the dog pawing at the door. After knocking several times and still receiving no reply except from the animal, Hamblen and Wayne forced the door open. They were greeted by a frail hound, his bones all but sticking through his skin. After petting the creature and after his eyes adjusted to the dark room, Hamblen spotted the cabin's human occupant. On a bed, in a far corner of the small one-room house, lay a man. He had obviously been dead for quite a while.

Approaching him, Hamblen noted a look of peacefulness on the man's face. All around him were old photos of what Hamblen guessed were family members. He also spotted an open Bible lying beside the bed. After saying a short prayer, he turned to Wayne and the others and assuredly stated, "He has gone to a better home."

The hunting party buried the man beside his cabin, picked up what special belongings they could find for any relatives he might have, and brought the dog with them. Yet even after he had returned to Los Angeles and his busy schedule, Hamblen couldn't get the scene out of his mind. Finally, in an effort to pay tribute to the solitary man and to try to understand his final thoughts, Hamblen took up his pen and recorded his observations. Before he got up from his desk he had written a song called "This Ole House."

The story was a simple one of a man dying before he had completed the responsibilities of his life. There were so many things he had left undone, so many minor chores he had meant to complete. When death caught up with him, those things were still waiting to be accomplished. Yet rather than be saddened by a broken chair that hadn't been mended or a roof that still leaked, he had died peacefully. Hamblen was struck by the fact that those things didn't matter. As he looked at his own life, he also discovered that most of what had caused him stress didn't matter either. What did matter was doing the Lord's will now, while he still had time. Then, when he met his Lord face to face, he would have accomplished the important things in his life. Thus, rather than being a song about a man dying alone, "This Ole House" became a tribute to the joy of living for Christ on earth and meeting Him in glory.

It is doubtful that Hamblen foresaw his little song as much more than a unique personal testimony for himself and the men who had accompanied him on the hunting trip. Yet when he sang "This Ole House" on his radio program, the audience response was enormous. Fans wrote and called, demanding to know where they could purchase the record. Because of this demand, he recorded and released the song. Then, not only did he suddenly find this study in faith and priorities on the pop music hit parade, but he discovered that a string of secular artists were rushing to the studio to cut it too. Rosemary Clooney's version of "This Ole House" even hit #1 and stayed on top of the charts for three weeks. Recorded and performed countless times since then, "This Ole House" has become a standard in both country and popular music. In 1998 the Brian Setzer Orchestra, a modern swing-boogie band, put it on their million-selling compact disc.

Today, almost five decades after Hamblen spotted the cabin, the story of the man who died there alone has inspired millions of people to come to understand that the next world is just a heartbeat away. With this in mind, Christians can put into perspective the pressures, demands, and concerns of the moment and concentrate on the important business at hand. Certainly Stuart Hamblen learned that lesson and used it in his own life. Until he died in 1989, this born-again Christian went about God's work as if each day were his last, and in this way he prepared to meet his Maker. When he died, Hamblen might have needed to clean his desk and mow the yard, but ... did it really matter?

This World Is Not My Home

Much of the magic to be found in the work of Albert E. Brumley consists of the use of elementary words that explain incredibly complex thoughts set to simple melodies that lend themselves to easy harmonies. Thus his music doesn't just make a spiritual impact, it is also fun to sing. This is probably the reason that once he devoted his life full time to his music, his songs spread like lightning across the United States.

In the days before World War II Brumley and his work were barely recognized, but by the time the United States began fighting in Korea, he was probably the best-known inspirational songwriter in the world. A great deal of his fame had to do with his understanding of what made a song popular. There seems to be little doubt that if he had chosen to, he could have used his talents to pen endless numbers of country or pop standards. He was a genius who knew that in order to have his work remembered and embraced, he had to keep his songs simple and direct. He also had to develop a theme that brought either greater understanding or joy, or both. In other words, with the popularity there had to be substance.

Living through two major World Wars, seeing so many die of disease before the advent of modern medicines, and observing the fortunes of millions destroyed by the Great Depression, Brumley was well aware of the frailty of life. He was equally certain of the sureness of death. Thus he often looked beyond earth to glory in order to give people an understanding of the rewards of faith. His songs "I'll Fly Away," "I'll Meet You in the Morning," "I'm Bound for That City," and "I'm Bound for the Land of Canaan" all centered on getting to heaven, as did "This World Is Not My Home."

Although it is interjected into the lyrics so subtly that few recognize it, a very complex and troubling facet of human nature—the desire to amass fame and fortune—is the basis of "This World Is Not My Home." Brumley understood that when the final curtain fell and one's days on earth were finished, money and power meant nothing. He fully grasped the fact that life on earth was just a transitory period. What lay just beyond death offered a fullness of glory and riches that would make those of this life seem trivial. But he also knew that this wasn't a reward that everyone would receive. One had to embrace Jesus Christ and His salvation to receive it. With these thoughts in mind, Albert penned four stanzas and a chorus addressing a wealth of Christian theology in just a few words.

First and foremost, "This World Is Not My Home" fully embraces the theme of Jesus as a friend. There is a natural long-ing to be with close friends. People will drive thousands of miles to renew special friendships. For Brumley, whose close friends numbered in the hundreds, his Lord was the one Friend the writer knew he couldn't do without. Using the chorus to anchor this thought, he then built four stanzas that spoke of rewards in heaven, a reunion of loved ones, eternal life, joy, shouting, victory, and praise. In short, Brumley not only painted a glowing picture of heaven but also defined the beauty of a spiritual relationship with God here on earth.

"This World Is Not My Home" has been recorded count-less times. Perhaps more than any other Brumley tune, it has also been rearranged to fit into country, southern gospel, black gospel, pop, contemporary Christian, and even choral work. Although simple and straightforward, this song has been heard in "high church" settings, as well as sung out of shaped-note hymnals by those who worship in brush arbor temples. No matter what one's station in life is, this song is a powerful testament to the promise of a life beyond this one for those who embrace faith.

By the time Albert Brumley died in 1977, more than two hundred major recording artists had cut at least one of his sacred songs. Not only had his music become staples for the Cathedrals, the Chuck Wagon Gang, the Blackwood Brothers, the Happy Goodmans, and scores of other gospel groups, but it had also been performed and recorded by the likes of Ray Charles, the Boston Pops Orchestra, Charley Pride, Merle Haggard, Chet Atkins, Floyd Cramer, Elvis Presley, and Red Foley. Of all the men who composed strictly gospel music, Brumley has had his work heard more than any other.

When Brumley finally left this world for his eternal home, when he at last got to sing with the heavenly choir, the song of sweetest praise they were singing had probably been written by their newest member. Most gospel music historians believe that even the angels sing Brumley's songs.

Through It All

Andraé Crouch has always been optimistic. He is constantly looking on the bright side of every situation. For most of his life he has looked at people and quickly discovered more things he liked than things he didn't like. When he recently took over the pastorate of a church in the inner city, he didn't see the problems, he saw the potential. By dwelling on the positive, he has been able to quickly shake off disappointments and find ways of turning failures into successes. Yet in very bad times even Crouch has needed the help of other Christians to guide him back to the Lord.

Early in his career, at a time when only a few gospel music lovers in California knew his name, Crouch and his group spent most of their nights performing in small churches and depending on love offerings to pay their expenses. Often they discovered some congregations didn't have a lot of the giving kind of love. More often than not, times were tough. While many in the group grumbled, Andraé was busy smiling, singing, and looking forward to the next chance to praise the Lord. To him even the lean days were wonderful.

One reason for his positive attitude was young love. He had fallen hard for a singer who often worked with him. He thought she was the most nearly perfect woman the Lord had ever created. When he couldn't be with her, he would spend hours thinking about how special their lives were going to be when they became a couple. He was sure that God had placed her with him to complete his life. As it turned out, the most important things to come of this relationship were not marriage and family but a song and a deeper understanding of how to walk with God.

"I was really fond of this young lady," Crouch recalled. "I had even purchased a ring. We were working three days at a church in Northern California and I had picked out that time to ask her to be my companion in life. On the first night we worked in the church, she didn't show up. No one knew why, and I wondered what had happened. She wasn't there the next night either."

By the third and final evening at the church, Crouch was frantic. But when he saw the woman he loved finally walk through the door, he thought his prayers had been answered. She had a huge smile on her face, and he had never seen her look more beautiful. Before the service began she excitedly brought everyone together to announce that she was in love and was going to be married. As a matter of fact, she had been away from the services because she had spent the last two days with the man who was to be her future husband.

Andraé was crushed. As he felt the ring in his pocket, he wanted to die. Suddenly the man who always saw the bright side of everything could see only darkness. After the final performance of the week, he talked to no one and drove five hours straight to his home. Distraught and broken in spirit, he didn't know how he could go on. He wanted to be alone; he didn't want anyone to bother him. Yet it wasn't to be. As he walked into his living room his phone rang. Picking up the receiver, he heard a familiar voice.

"Albie Pearson, a ballplayer for the Los Angeles Angels, had called me," Crouch remembered. "The first words out of his mouth were that he had been praying for me. He didn't have any idea as to what had happened, he just thought I needed some prayer and encouragement. As we talked, he told me that God would take me through the fresh grass growing in abundance in the valley, as well as the fresh grass on the mountain top."

Although Pearson couldn't have known it, by using the highest and lowest points on God's earth as reference points, he inspired Crouch not only to not give up on love and life but to write a song as well. Within minutes Crouch was at the piano.

"I was weeping," he explained, "and I was thinking about what Albie had told me. Then I got to thinking about what David went through. Yet even as he went through the bad times, God's rod directed him, and His staff comforted him. Using these things as my inspiration and setting them against what I was feeling at the time, I wrote the first two verses of 'Through It All.' But even though I knew that it needed one more, I couldn't get a third verse at that time."

It would take a natural disaster for the writer to be able to finish his song. Out of the rumble and ruins of an earthquake came the vision for the final stanza of "Through It All."

"The night after the terrible Los Angeles quake," Crouch remembered, "I felt so thankful. So many things in the city had been destroyed, but God had allowed everything to stay in place at our home. Nothing was hurt at all. This gave me the inspiration to finish the song."

In truth it would take longer for him to get over his broken heart than it would the city of Los Angeles to get over the earthquake. The scars of his broken love ran very deep. But the lessons he learned from that experience are some of the greatest he has ever known. He recalls them each time he sings "Through It All."

"I thought I would never recover from my broken heart," he admits. "Yet I came to realize that it is a blessing to know that God has put other people on our hearts. Albie Pearson called me at just the moment I needed him and showed me the opposites of life. He pointed out to me how God directs us and our lives and that even when we don't understand, we must learn to trust Him."

Like so many songs, "Through It All" was written as therapy—a bridge over individual pain and loss. Yet when Andraé Crouch shared his music with others, the intimate nature of the song didn't get in the way of sharing the power of God with them. Millions grew to think of "Through It All" as their story. In a very real sense, it is the story of all people who have come to lean on God through both the good and the bad times.

Turn Your Radio On

Albert E. Brumley, a son of tenant farmers, was born in the Indian Territory in 1905.

During his early years, there were two things that made Brumley stand out. One was his musical ability. He could sing and read music better than most adults. The other was his style of dress. While he wore bib overalls, just like all the other boys in Rock Island, Oklahoma, he also sported a tie.

In 1922, at the age of sixteen, Albert attended a meeting that dramatically changed his own life and the lives of millions of others as well. While at a singing school session to learn more about how to harmonize properly, Brumley met men who had written some of the music they were teaching. A thought struck him: *If they can do it, maybe I can too.*

Although he had quit school after the tenth grade, Brumley believed the only way to really succeed at something was to understand how others had done it well. With these thoughts guiding him, he sought out the work of the very best song-writers. Over several months he learned in minute detail every Eugene Bartlett song he could find. He not only memorized the melodies but also studied the harmonies, the words, and the subtle facets of each arrangement. Through Bartlett's work he began to understand that a gospel music song was more than a nice set of lyrics coupled with a tune. To write something very special and inspirational, a composer had to literally find the perfect marriage of words and music. Through his study of

Bartlett, he came to believe that the most important part of this union was the way a song was metered and phrased.

The first song Albert wrote was "I Can Hear Them Singing Over There." For an amateur songwriter it was a remarkable piece of work. Yet rather than alter his life, it only served to entertain his friends. Unable to find a publisher for the song, Brumley still spent his days in the cotton fields.

During the early part of the century, poor farm boys just didn't have much self-confidence. Humility was driven into most of them from the day they were born. Pride of any kind was seen as a sin. Hence most boys rarely left the farm to seek out their dreams. Albert Brumley might have suffered this same fate if his "I Can Hear Them Singing Over There" had not finally been published in the *Gates of Glory* songbook. Using this one song as his own inspiration, he packed his bags and made a long train trip to Hartford, Arkansas, to meet his mentor.

It took a great deal of courage for Brumley to walk up to Eugene Bartlett and introduce himself. Yet he didn't stop there. They had no more than shaken hands when young Brumley exclaimed, "I hear that you'll teach a fella how to sing and how to write music. I've come to learn, and I understand I don't have to have any money."

The first part was true, Bartlett did have a school where he taught composition, but he couldn't teach, feed, house, and clothe every person who wanted to study with him. Yet he was touched by Albert's honest approach. Rather than do the logical thing and turn Albert away, he invited the young man to stay in his own home and study by his side. As Brumley would later say, "Telling me to go to his house meant more to me than being invited to the White House to live with the president!"

Bartlett not only gave the best musical training a wannabe gospel songwriter could have, but he also shared his trust, his wisdom, and his friendship. When Brumley left Hartford and began his own ministry of song, Bartlett's fingerprints could be seen on almost all of his work.

Just a decade after making the trip to Arkansas, Brumley had become America's best-known gospel music writer. His work had been taken far and wide in hundreds of songbooks and through the voices of scores of artists via radio and records. Seemingly overnight almost everyone in the country had heard and could sing such Brumley tunes as "I'll Fly Away," "I'll Meet You in the Morning," "Jesus, Hold My Hand," and "If We Never Meet Again." On every gospel music show on both local and national radio, it seemed that at least one of Brumley's songs was being played.

By 1937 Brumley had moved to Missouri, started his own publishing company, and emerged not only as one of the country's best songwriters but also as a top draw at singing schools and conventions. The gospel songs he was writing had become so popular that he literally had groups holding up recording sessions so they could be the first to cut the newest Albert Brumley song.

His friends and neighbors were naturally proud. They also tried to be aware of who was singing which Brumley song. Many would tune in to hear quartets such as the Stamps-American, Stamps-Ozark, and the Speer Family just to check if they were using a Brumley original on that broadcast. If one of the groups sang one of his songs, there was a rush to the telephone.

"They would call me," Brumley later explained, "whenever they heard anyone singing one of my songs. The first thing they would always say was, 'Albert, turn your radio on.'"

It didn't take long for this simple phrase to inspire him to write another song. Not only had his own music spread quickly and become well known because of the power of radio, but religious outreach in general had also been mightily propelled over the airwaves. Until radio there had never been an invention that had made reaching lost souls so easy and effective. As Brumley saw it, radio was an even more important tool for Christ than the printing press. After all, everyone could listen to radio, but only those who could read could use books. A lot of folks must have agreed with Brumley, because by 1938 "Turn Your Radio On" had become the writer's best-known song.

The Stamps Quartet and Blackwood Brothers quickly picked up the song, and hundreds of other gospel artists did too, many using it as their radio program theme song. Through wartime and into the fifties "Turn Your Radio On" was one of gospel music's most recognized gospel standards. Yet by the sixties, with the advent of television and the sounds of rock music, the popularity of the Brumley classic seemed to be on the wane.

And then in 1971 Ray Stevens was looking for a new vehicle to place him back at the top of the charts. Known as a novelty singer and writer, the gifted Stevens, a Georgia native, decided to turn his attention to his own gospel roots. He had grown up listening to the Blackwood Brothers. Moving into the studio, playing all the instruments and supplying all the vocals himself, Ray tried to update the old southern gospel sound he had heard and sung as a child. The one song and arrangement he left intact was "Turn Your Radio On."

Because music was driven by being played on the radio, Ray's Barnaby label took a chance and released this overtly religious song as a single. The results were monumental. In the age of acid rock and Woodstock, "Turn Your Radio On" raced onto the rock charts while also becoming the hit that paved the way for Stevens' successful move to country music. Millions who had never heard of southern gospel music and had never been to church quickly learned the words and music.

In 1972 Ray Stevens' pop-country hit "Turn Your Radio On" reaffirmed what Albert Brumley had recognized almost four decades before. Now, more than twenty-five years after Stevens' discovery, what Brumley wrote in 1937 still remains true: radio has been and is the most important vehicle for spreading the popularity of gospel music. Thanks to radio, southern gospel, African-American gospel, and country gospel gained a national audience, and, in the process, radio also paved the way for gospel music to influence all other forms of music. It was even radio that jump-started a Christian revival powered by gospel music. Today you can still hear the sounds of heaven and the good news of salvation when you "turn your radio on."

The Unclouded Day

*J*osiah Alwood could probably identify with the apostle Paul. Alwood, an ordained minister in the church of the United Brethren of Christ, spent years in Christian service as a circuit-riding preacher. On horseback he would journey great distances to tiny Ohio churches to deliver sermons and teach Bible studies. These small congregations, many of which met only once a month, waited anxiously for Alwood's visit. To as many as a half dozen churches, he was their connection with the Word. In rural areas, where most people didn't even read, he gave believers and the wandering lost their only contact with the Scriptures.

Throughout the 1870s and 1880s, Alwood spent hours each day alone with his horse. He was a man of peace who had been called to travel untamed backroads for the Lord. He often went weeks without seeing his home or his family. Many Sundays he rode through driving rain or blinding snow to get from his morning pastorate to the evening church service he led in the next county. He braved not only weather but also bandits and wild animals. Although he never complained to his flocks, his life was difficult, and his loneliness must often have been overwhelming.

Alwood was at the end of another circuit on a cold, clear night in late 1880s. It had been weeks since he had seen his family, and he was eager to get home. Nevertheless, after the evening service many of the members of the church stopped to visit with him about matters of faith and Scripture, delaying his leaving. The pastor, ever patient with his parishioners, stayed late into the evening, answering questions, addressing concerns, and taking a moment to pray for each troubled soul. When he finally saddled his horse and headed down the dusty trail toward his own home, it was late and the world seemed deep in sleep.

With nothing to keep him company and unable to read in the darkness, Alwood began to think of the sermons he had preached over the past few weeks. He wondered if any of them had touched a soul or caused a person to accept the Lord. As must have even happened to the apostle Paul when he was tired and alone with a burden and a mission too great to bear, he began to doubt whether the calling he had followed was worth the effort. Exhausted, still many miles from home and well behind schedule, the preacher seemed to have only one thing in his favor. On this night no storm clouds loomed on the horizon and no cold wind tore through his clothing. As Alwood looked up, he even caught a glimpse of a full moon coming up in a clear sky. He smiled, knowing that all the way home his path would be lit.

Although he never understood just where it came from, as he traveled that night Josiah began to hum a tune. The melody came easy, like a long-forgotten song from childhood, but it seemed new to him. Try as he might, Alwood couldn't trace the tune back to any moment in his life. After humming it for several miles, he began to try to come up with words to match the melody. He had only to look back at the cloudless heavens for his inspiration.

As tired and sleepy as he was, Alwood was suddenly filled with an incredible energy and enthusiasm. An optimism surged through his heart, and joy filled his voice. Although no people were awake to hear him, with only startled animals making up his audience, he began to sing at the top of his lungs:

O they tell me of a home far beyond the skies,
O they tell me of a home far away;
O they tell me of a home where no storm clouds rise,
O they tell me of an unclouded day.

For Alwood the words to his song were at least a bit auto-biographical. At the mercy of the elements, constantly away from his own family, he knew firsthand the joy of coming home. As he sang he must have been overcome by trying to compare the peace and happiness he found from just walking into his own front door with the awesome emotions he knew he would experience when he crossed over to be with his Savior in his heavenly home. On that night, when he finally arrived home, he woke his wife and asked her to sit beside him at their tiny pump organ and listen to the song he called "The Unclouded Day."

"The Unclouded Day" was first published in 1890 and soon became a favorite in rural churches across the Midwest. Unlike most hymns of the period, there was a folk-music feel about "The Unclouded Day." It seemed to sound best when sung by untrained, simple people. Perhaps because of the song's direct, elemental, and rather straightforward style, few city churches latched onto it. Yet the fact that the song was unsophisticated and that it seemed meant to be sung in clear air while viewing nature's majesty probably kept it from being lost in the back of dusty hymnals.

In the thirties, with the advent of radio and gospel music driven by quartets, "The Unclouded Day" went uptown. Because it was easy to sing and featured an opportunity for wonderful four-part harmonies and because its message appealed to those going through the hard times of the Great Depression, scores of local groups made it a standard of their performances. Because of this new exposure, "The Unclouded Day" became not only a favorite congregational hymn but also one of the most chosen funeral songs of the period.

When contemporary Christian music took the nation by storm in the seventies and more emphasis was placed on "new" sounds, it seemed that the now century-old hymn would be forgotten. Churches had changed, music was more sophisticated, few could read shaped notes, and young folks just didn't seem to cotton to the older gospel songs. Dropped from most books, all but forgotten in most areas, "The Unclouded Day" seemed as outdated as the circuit-riding preacher who wrote it. The song might have been lost altogether if it had not been for a country music star using it to cheer up an audience having hard times making ends meet.

In 1987 Willie Nelson traveled to Illinois to perform at a benefit for farmers who had been caught in a death grip by a bad economy. Seemingly overnight thousands of family farms had been lost because of low prices and high interest. Nationally televised, Nelson's Farm Aid concert featured all of his hits, a host of guest acts, and several tributes to the American farmer. A surprise to many, the singer added something else too. Himself a product of the Depression, to end his performance Nelson reached back to a song from his youth in Abbott, Texas. Willie's hopeful message for the future was wrapped in the words of J.K. Alwood's hymn, "The Unclouded Day."

Since Nelson's performance a number of gospel groups have added "The Unclouded Day" to their concert performances and recorded it again. The horseback-riding preacher who once wondered if he was touching anyone with his words is still touching millions today with his vision of what heaven will be.

Until Then

Although they are rarely found in hymnbooks, the gospel songs of Stuart Hamblen seem to remain as popular with Christians today as when he wrote them almost five decades ago. One reason may be that he was a writer of popular hit-parade music long before he turned to writing gospel songs. Because much of his living depended on royalty revenue, he had to know what people liked. Yet the fact that he understood the desires of the mass market cannot be the only reason his gospel songs remain so fresh today. Without a doubt there is something special in his gospel songs that isn't in other songs he wrote, such as "(I Won't Go Huntin', Jake.) But I'll Go on Chasin' Women" and "(Remember Me.) I'm the One Who Loves You."

Timeless gospel music is not written according to a formula; it must be inspired. Hamblen's work drew from his own life, his conversion at a Billy Graham Crusade, and his desire to talk to his friends about Christ. Unlike his secular songs, which came from the thrill of a moment, his religious work sprang from a well of endless joy. Thus the lasting power of songs such as "Until Then" is firmly rooted in their message and spirit. These classics not only make people listen, they also make people consider the worth of their own lives.

Of all of Hamblen's classics, "Until Then" is probably the most simple, yet it may also be the most profound. The song's lyrics are a study of his past, present, and future, as well as his deep sorrow about his past sinful ways and his joy at finding true peace and contentment through salvation.

Although he was the son of a preacher, when he moved to California to find his fortune in show business, Stuart Hamblen quickly became one of Hollywood's most notorious partyers. While somehow maintaining his career, he burned the candle at both ends. This successful actor, singer, and radio host often sat in bars with the world's most famous stars, then spent the day betting the ponies at the track with the elite of Los Angeles. The songs he wrote during his two decades of boisterous behavior reflected his lifestyle. His songs and his world were filled with drinking, cheating, and lying. In a very real sense, everything he wrote celebrated how not to live a Christian life.

Yet under the wild exterior was a caring man with a gentle heart. Although it would take his wife, Suzy, more than fifteen years to help bring the best of Stuart to the surface, she knew her husband had the potential to fulfill a higher calling. Even while many of her friends felt this dedicated Christian woman was wasting her time waiting for her husband to change, she kept praying. She had the faith to believe that he would someday come to know the Lord, and she would wait until then.

When Hamblen finally did attend a Billy Graham Crusade and was saved, he realized not only the waste of the many years he had lived a sinful life but also the incredible strength and faith his wife had displayed as she stayed by him through the years of bad times. With her as an example of Christian dedication at its best, he gave himself completely to God.

He prayed, studied the Bible, and never missed a chance to share his story with others. His radio shows began to center on Christian outreach. He spent months on the road with Billy Graham and other ministers, giving his testimony. He worked with Christian youth groups and witnessed on the movie lots and rodeo circuits.

Many of Stuart's old friends simply couldn't understand his new life. In their view, the fun and adventure had been stripped from him; yet he was still smiling. So profound was their confusion that many came to his home and asked questions, trying to uncover the motive behind his radical shift in priorities. Yet they often left still mystified. They just couldn't understand the big picture. They couldn't understand how giving up something that seemed like so much fun could lead to something that appeared to him—but not to them—so much greater.

"Until Then" was Stuart's way of admitting that he didn't have all the answers, but he had the faith that someday he would. He was now satisfied to live in the light, staying away from the sinful world, until the day God would call him home and explain it all to him. This was the message he had first seen in his wife's life, and now he wanted those who knew him to see it in his.

To Hamblen's credit, many of his former partying friends were eventually moved by his witness. Many of them came to know the same Lord and embrace the same life that had so dramatically changed Hamblen. A large part of their conversion experience came about because their friend continued to support them and pray for them as his wife had once done for him. He never gave up.

Stuart Hamblen died in 1989. His passing was noted by hundreds of newspapers around the world. The focus of the obituaries was not his movies, his radio shows, or his days as a Hollywood partyer; rather, the stories centered on his gospel music. In death, as in the latter half of his life, Stuart touched souls with his faith. With his music still being recorded and sung, he will no doubt continue his mighty Christian witness until the Lord calls all of us home.

Victory in Jesus

*B*orn in the Ozark Hills of Missouri in 1885, Eugene Monroe Bartlett was a child prodigy. Blessed with a strong singing voice and a bright mind, at a time when few boys graduated from eighth grade, Bartlett studied at Hall-Moody Institute and William Jewell Academy. Trained as a music teacher, he hit the road in 1914 and never looked back. Journeying from town to town, from church to church, and from singing convention to singing convention, Bartlett touched thousands with his talent, his voice, and his dramatic presentations.

Not satisfied just to perform and teach the old familiar standards, he began to write his own hymns. Framed in the southern gospel tradition that had been a part of his youth, E.M., as he was often called, brought to his songs the emotions, fears, and complete life experiences of the men and women he taught. Some of his compositions, such as "I Heard My Mother Call My Name in Prayer," "Everybody Will Be Happy Over There," and "He Will Remember Me," spoke of families' hope and faith as few hymns ever had.

In 1918, while living in the tiny Arkansas community of Hartford, Bartlett built upon his own writing experience by founding the Hartford Music Company. He used this company as a forum to publish not only his own songs but also those of other up-and-coming writers of the day. Successful beyond his wildest dreams, the singer, writer, and now publisher could have cut back on his busy schedule, spent more time with his family, and enjoyed the blessings brought by his work. Yet, rather than give in to the temptation of an easier life, he continued to go out into the small churches throughout the South and Midwest, sharing his music, his testimony, and his faith. In his own mind he was responding to a call to serve his Lord.

Even though the travel was often hard and the time spent away from home was difficult, E.M. seemed to be able to do with grace and ease everything he attempted. Nothing bothered him, nothing stopped him, and there were no challenges that derailed his mission or his faith. While he was revered by tens of thousands across the country and his songs were sung by millions, a few people wondered if he could sustain his faith if he were ever faced with a major challenge. Yet as he rolled along, as his voice continued to soar, as he effortlessly wrote great gospel songs and funny little odes such as "Take an Old Cold Tater and Wait," it seemed that he would always travel the easy road.

During the last years of the Great Depression, Bartlett had reached his fifties and should have been slowing down. Even with trains and cars, travel was difficult. The many trips to backroad churches and small-town radio stations must have been very difficult for him. Yet, instead of cutting back, he continued to make long trips from his Arkansas home across Oklahoma, Texas, Missouri, and Louisiana to share the gospel message with thousands each month.

In 1939 the combination of hard work and fatigue finally caught up with him. A major stroke left him partially paralyzed and unable to perform or travel. Confined to his home, tended to by his family and friends, the man who had once worked tirelessly for weeks on end now had difficulty moving across his own bedroom. Friends and family were deeply concerned. They wondered how he would respond to a world that had once had no boundaries but now was cut down to the size of a few rooms.

Contrary to the fears of many, Bartlett seemed to be bothered little by the affliction he suffered. He rarely paused to reflect on his own pain or limitations and simply got on with the business of pushing forward with the challenges that faced him. Taken off the road by the results of his stroke, he spent time studying the Bible, visiting with his family, and considering his many blessings. Rather than be driven to doubts, he seemed to grow stronger in his faith even as his body grew weaker each day. And as if to prove to all those around him that the faith they saw in him was genuine, that he really didn't feel as if his God had let him down or deserted him, he struggled to express his own views of life, hope, faith, and the future in a new song.

For Bartlett the process of writing was now as monumental as climbing Mt. Everest. Nothing came easy. Just attempting to relate his own thoughts to others wore him out. Ideas that once formed instantly and were immediately transformed to music and lyrics now seemed to inch along. Words didn't burst out now. They had to be pulled from a mind bent on shutting down in a body that was little more than a shell of the vibrant vessel it had once been. Undaunted, Bartlett pushed forward, trying to meet the challenge of expressing himself in the restraints of new parameters. With a joy usually seen only on a child's face as he masters his first step, the writer put together a phrase, a line, and a verse. Finally, after he had expended more effort and sweat on a song than he had ever done before, Bartlett's new testimony of faith and hope was spelled out in a song about healing, power, and victory.

"Victory in Jesus" was immediately published by the James D. Vaughan publishing company, then picked up by a host of others, including Albert W. Brumley and Stamps Music. Yet the writer of the song didn't live long enough to learn what his final composition would come to mean to millions.

On January 25, 1941, Eugene Monroe Bartlett died. He was just fifty-five years old. Yet the last song he wrote, the final note of a remarkable career, is now the one that defines not only his gifts to Christian music but also the man himself. In the face of a stroke that left him only a shell of his former self, when his horizon had been whittled down from a wide world of travel and acclaim to just a few small rooms, looking toward a future that offered little but pain and suffering, Bartlett saw victory. Best of all, he not only saw this wonderful and glorious triumph for himself, but he also shared it with the world. That is why his final curtain call is still bringing people to Jesus today.

Walk Dem Golden Stairs

In 1948 a Springfield, Missouri, quartet made up of Bob Hubbard, Bill Matthews, Monty Matthews, and Cully Holt got together to sing a few barbershop quartet numbers. They blended so well they chose a name, the Jordanaires, and began to sing gospel and spiritual music at a few local churches. By 1949 they had polished their act to such a great extent that they were invited to be guests on the *Grand Ole Opry*. Yet just a few months after their Nashville debut it appeared that the Ozark foursome was headed for obscurity. Hubbard was drafted into the armed forces, and Bill Matthews was hit with an illness that was so serious it forced him to quit the group. If the Jordanaires had ended there, the feel and sound of gospel and popular music might have been much different today.

However, as Providence would have it, two graduates of the famed Stamps singing school were looking for work at the very instant that Monty Matthews and Cully Holt needed new singing partners. The addition of Gordon Stoker and Hoyt Hawkins kept the quartet going and paved the way for some monumental musical history. This story began in earnest when the Jordanaires signed a record deal and started backing up Red Foley on radio.

"What set us apart at that time," Stoker remembered, "was that we sang spirituals. White quartets of the time just didn't sing black spirituals. We loved them, and our audiences did too. During our early years some of our most requested numbers were 'Swing Low, Sweet Chariot,' 'Search Me, Lord,' and

'Joshua Fit the Battle of Jericho.' We even cut 'Peace in the Valley' before Red Foley did."

The fact that the Jordanaires liked the feel of songs by black writers and artists shouldn't have been a surprise. All of them had grown up listening to choirs of black singers. They loved the freedom of expression that was so much a part of the spiritual sound. And as they quickly found out, so did pop-music audiences.

"We made a trip to New York to work on Arthur Godfrey's show," Stoker recalled, "and we sang the old Negro spiritual 'Dig a Little Deeper.' That song literally stopped the show. Godfrey came over to the mike and said, 'Boys, I've never heard anything like that. I want you to sing again.'

"A little while later we were called in to back up the wonderful Mahalia Jackson on a song. When we finished, she looked over at us almost in disbelief. She told the whole studio, 'I wanna sing with those boys again.' She did, too!"

Mahalia wasn't the only one who liked their unique style and special blend. Soon Eddy Arnold, Tennessee Ernie Ford, Hank Snow, and Jimmy Wakely were wanting to have the Jordanaires work their recording sessions. By 1956 the foursome not only had a successful career in their own right but were the most popular back-up artists in the recording industry as well. Just when the group thought nothing could make their lives any better, a young man from Memphis was signed to an RCA recording contract.

"From the very start we worked Elvis's sessions," Stoker explained. "And when the sessions were over, we often hung around and sang gospel songs for several more hours. Elvis's favorite music was gospel, and he loved to sing spirituals."

Not only did the Jordanaires find themselves on Presley's hit records; they also toured with him, appeared with him on almost every national television guest show, and traveled to Los Angeles to sing on his movie soundtracks and even appear in his films. By 1958, though it wasn't for their gospel records, the Jordanaires had become the best-known southern gospel group in the world.

"Even though we were working with Elvis, Jim Reeves, Patsy Cline, Ernie Ford, Ricky Nelson, and a host of others," Stoker explained, "we were still cutting records of our own too. So, although it seemed like it to a lot people, we hadn't given up gospel. We were singing gospel music to more people than we ever had. We just weren't singing to the audiences of the rest of the quartets at that time."

It was while cutting a new album that the inspiration for one of their best-remembered and most popular songs was born. "In one session," Stoker recalled, "our bass singer, Cully Holt, began to talk to Monty Matthews about going to heaven. Cully kept talking about walking the golden stairs to the pearly gates. Although he was not a songwriter, and to my knowledge never wrote another song, he went home and put words and music to his thoughts. When he was finished, he brought the song back to us. I knew when I first heard it that 'Walk Dem Golden Stairs' was great."

Holt's "Stairs" gave the Jordanaires a song that fit their style perfectly. The words, the message, and even the beat reflected the black spiritual sound that had set the Jordanaires apart from other southern gospel groups of the era. Once they cut it, the quartet began to use it in all their shows and even sang "Stairs" in the studio when they were warming up their voices.

"By 1960 a lot of people were doing the song," Stoker recalled, "so I don't know if Elvis had picked it up from us or somewhere else. Yet when we were called in to do a gospel album with Elvis, we began to sing a little bit of 'Walk Dem

Golden Stairs.' During a break Elvis joined in. As soon as he learned the words, he decided that he had to use it on the album we were cutting. I didn't believe it was going to happen. His manager, Tom Parker, had instructed RCA to use only songs that were in the public domain. He didn't want to have to pay out any royalties to songwriters or publishers. So when Elvis decided he wanted to do 'Walk Dem Golden Stairs,' I guess I should have spoken up and told Colonel Parker that Cully had written it and that Ben Speer Music owned the rights. But I decided to keep my mouth shut. I knew that Ben could use the money a lot more than Tom Parker."

The session went through the night, and Elvis and the group didn't put the final touches on the album until well past sunrise. As they walked out, Stoker brought the other members of the quartet together and made them vow to keep the fact that "Stairs" was not in the public domain a secret. Stoker then got Ben Speer on the phone.

"Ben was so excited," Stoker recalled, "but I cautioned him not say anything to anyone. If Colonel Parker found out that Ben Speer Music owned the rights, he would have the recording of 'Stairs' cut from the album. So for months we all sat on the news. Finally, after the album 'His Hand in Mine' hit the market and was selling well, Ben called RCA and informed them that he owned the rights to 'Walk Dem Golden Stairs.' For the first time since I had met him, the Colonel had been outfoxed. It was wonderful to see Ben Speer Music get a piece of the pie and Cully Holt's song become one of the best-known gospel songs in the world."

"Walk Dem Golden Stairs" became a signature song for the Jordanaires. Still a fan favorite, it was also the song that best spotlighted the group's unique blend of southern gospel and Negro spiritual music. While the Jordanaires are now mainly remembered as the world's most recorded back-up singers, "Walk Dem Golden Stairs" reminds those in the gospel field that this quartet did more than just back famous artists. Although there are many other reasons why the Gospel Music Association recently elected the Jordanaires to its Hall of Fame, maybe the best reason is that they were the first to bring gospel's black and white roots together.

We'll Soon Be Done With Troubles and Trials

 $\mathscr{F}$ ew men know more about troubles and trials than did the Reverend Cleavant Derricks. The kindly minister spent much of his life pastoring the poor, the outcast, and the forgotten. He preached to those who were often and unfairly viewed as second-class citizens. Week after week and in sermon after sermon he sought to inspire a people who seemed to have few opportunities in their own land. He worked with little rest, often walked miles to visit sick neighbors, and lived without things he needed so that others in his flock might have what they needed. He was a Christian who lived by the challenge of reaching the "least" of those around him. Although eloquent in speech and wise in his understanding of the Scripture, he never held himself above those who turned to him for help and guidance.

To understand the places where Derricks toiled, one must realize that the rural South of the first half of the 1900s was a region that offered few chances for its poor people. The cycle of poverty repeated itself again and again, generation after generation. For black people such as Derricks and those in his church, the opportunities were especially rare. For most of these people there were no steady jobs, no higher education, and no equal rights or fair representation. A huge segment of the commercial and entertainment world was cut off from African-Americans. They were not allowed to eat in restaurants, go to the best theaters, or even play baseball in the major leagues. When *Gone With the Wind* premiered in Atlanta, Hattie McDaniel, who went on to win an Academy Award for her role in the movie, was not even allowed to attend the movie's opening. Such were the hard realities of life.

Cleavant Derricks never understood why the world he had been born into was not fair. He knew things could be different for a man of his intelligence and talent in the North. Yet he didn't leave his people or his calling. He also never tried to win acceptance into the white society that surrounded him. He was proud of who he was—a Christian, a man of God who was black. He drew upon his own pride to minister to others. It was through his efforts to inspire his own people's faith in God, sense of worth in themselves, and belief that in heaven all are equal that the Rev., as he liked to be called, not only put into words and music the thoughts and experiences of African-Americans of the time but also deeply touched millions of people of all other races.

Although the words now seem to relate the thoughts of an old man facing death, "We'll Soon Be Done With Troubles and Trials" was written when Derricks was a young pastor. In his effort to find answers for his own people's oppression, he turned to heaven as the model for the way God wanted all people to be treated. Although completely hopeful in tone and delivery, when this song was set against the backdrop of unabashed racism, its theme displayed the unrest and pain that existed for men and women on earth. If heaven represented peace, earth stood as a monument to suffering. So, while his song might have been talking about glory, in truth it was also preaching about the joy of living in a place where opportunities were equal and life was fair.

Perhaps because of the Depression, millions of poor white Americans also quickly embraced the song. By World War II, when all the nation's people were fighting against the most wicked type of racism, Derricks's song became one of America's most sung gospel music standards. Recorded by black and white groups in every part of the country, it was hard to find a gospel music radio program that didn't use it at least once a week.

For the Rev. the popularity of "We'll Soon Be Done With Troubles and Trials," along with his other two classics of the period—"Just a Little Talk With Jesus" and "When God Dips His Love in My Heart"—must have been bittersweet. As a man of God it thrilled him to know that so many were being inspired by his work, but as a writer he must have been saddened to know others were profiting from it. Derricks had sold the rights to future royalties to all three classics for a few songbooks for his congregation.

By the time Cleavant Derricks walked into a Nashville publishing house in 1977 hoping to find someone to listen to his latest compositions, his music had been a part of the southern gospel scene for four decades. Although his music was sung by everyone from the Cathedrals to the Blackwoods, few outside of the industry knew the Rev.

"I had the opportunity to meet him a couple of times," Cathedrals bass singer George Younce recalled. "He was such a gentleman. He came backstage and was very humble. Not very many people even knew who he was. Yet he was such a great writer. I always thought it was a shame that he wasn't out in the spotlight being recognized for the great songs he had given to the world."

In truth, Derricks cared little about the spotlight. He simply wanted to share the message of salvation and bring inspiration to those going through tough times. When other African-Americans tried to have him recognized as an important member of their race, the Rev. deflected much of the attention by simply stating that in God's eyes we are all members of the same family.

After a long life of troubles and trials, after a period of time when many criticized the preacher for not being more militant and demanding the money and fame due him, the rights to Derricks's song were won back for him by his friends. He was also placed in the spotlight on a record made with his family.

Derricks loved the chance to record his songs in his own style, but he also never regretted the many trials he had experienced along the way or the time he had spent in obscurity. Just two years after being recognized by the music world, he died. The promise he wrote about in his song was finally realized in his own life—Cleavant Derricks was through with all his troubles and trials and had a chance to sit down and rest a little while. No man deserved to sit beside Jesus any more than did the Rev.

Were You There?

There can be little doubt that much of what has been called gospel music can trace its roots back to Africa. The great traditions of song of the native tribes along that continent's West Coast were among the few things that slave traders couldn't steal from their captives. The beat, the harmonies, and the unique lead vocals were taken by the captured Africans to America. Once there, these songs were passed from generation to generation as a way of connecting with a place that had allowed their bodies and spirits to run free.

If there was a single place where the music of Africa and the message of salvation came together, it was in the area around Savannah, Georgia. There, on huge rice and cotton plantations, the sounds of men and women harmonizing in the fields brought an ironically peaceful atmosphere to an institution awash in sin. While the choral-like music might have signaled a sense of peace and contentment, the subjects the slave writers chose as the themes of their songs painted the true story of oppression.

The spiritual feel of *gulla* (African folk music) had been in place for hundreds of years. Yet, as the masters' traditions and beliefs became a part of the slaves' lives, the message of the songs changed. Through the salvation experience black slaves began to understand that there were two kinds of bondage—physical and spiritual. Because there was so little they could do about unchaining their bodies, these men and women vigorously sought freedom for their souls.

The Christian message was one that a person held in slavery could easily relate to. The Bible was filled with stories of God relating to slaves. Christ Himself taught that all of us are slaves to something. Thus, accepting Christ and fully embracing His message was usually easier for the slave than it was for the master. Ironically, in these times in the old South, the pupils often became the teachers. Many times it was the field workers or house servants—men and women who had no earthly possessions, no legal rights, and no social standing—who provided the model for Christian charity.

One of the ways these oppressed people spread the hope of a better life and the joy of salvation was by taking their traditional music and adapting it to Christian themes. Using the stories of Adam, Noah, Jonah, Elijah, and scores of other biblical figures, African-Americans created songs that explained these ancient experiences in ways everyone could understand. As you listen to "Joshua Fit the Battle" or "Swing Low, Sweet Chariot," you not only hear the story, but you see and feel it too. It is as if you have been transported by the music to the day and place of the actual events. Although musically untrained, these composers and their choirs gave birth to the greatest American music of that time. Sadly, for many years the spirituals of the South went all but unnoticed by scholars, scribes, and religious leaders. Yet their message could not be ignored forever.

Many of the spirituals that have survived until this day embrace the joy of being saved. The harmonies, the rhythms, and the phrasing naturally create excitement. These songs move the heart, mind, and body. Hands can't keep from clapping, feet can't keep from dancing, and voices can't keep from singing and shouting. Yet not all spirituals were upbeat and exuberant. Some reflected not only the trials of a Christian life but the pain of slavery as well. It was one of these songs that first found favor with the established church audience.

"Were You There (When They Crucified My Lord)?" moved the soul by asking the most haunting and personal questions of those who stood by and allowed God's Son to be crucified. Through the lyrics of "Were You There?" the unknown writer painted a picture with very simple and direct imagery. In each succeeding verse, the sights, sounds, and reality of the crucifixion were chillingly portrayed. Much more than any other song about the Cross and the day Christ died, "Were You There?" created a picture that lingered long after the final note and words had drifted away.

By the late 1800s "Were You There?" found its way out of the slave fields and small black churches and into mainstream worship services of white congregations. The arrangement, the pacing, and the tune were changed very little. The feel of the gulla music remained intact.

When a white congregation sang "Were You There?" for the first time, an important message was subtly passed along to all Christians: while the color of skin may vary from person to person, the color of a soul is the same. Thus, contrary to the thought of some whites, even uneducated slaves were worthy of salvation and, no less, of respect. Their experience could be a testimony for everyone, no matter what his or her background, social standing, race, or age might be.

Decades before the nation began to integrate churches and schools, spirituals—beginning with "Where You There?"—had already opened the country's doors to the black religious experience. There can be little doubt that these songs inspired writers of all colors to create gospel music, and they set in motion a salvation experience for countless souls who first felt the presence of Christ through songs such as "Were You There?"

In a way it is a shame that a face and a name cannot be put to such an important, ground-breaking song. Yet maybe the fact that spirituals were the joint cries and shouts of new Christians looking for the freedom that only God could bring them gives the message of this song much more impact. None of us were there in body when Christ died, but all of us need to go there in spirit. To understand the gift of salvation, each sinner must realize that he or she is a slave to the world; only then does seeing Christ on the cross make the impact of His freeing us from those bonds all the more real.

When God Dips His Love in My Heart

$\mathcal{I}$n 1977 Word Music's Nashville division captured an all but unknown voice in their Bellemeade Mansion studio. Surrounded by his family, encouraged by seventy years of Christian service, for the first time Cleavant Derricks sang his own compositions for a world that had been singing them for more than four decades. For several days the elderly African-American minister worked with producer Aaron Brown to reconstruct the feel of the deeply spiritual songs that had been born in his heart through his experiences. Overlooked, underappreciated, and almost forgotten for many years, Derricks finally gained a place in the spotlight. The fact that it took so long for him to be recognized only serves to underscore just how much his music has meant to millions for generations.

As he sang in that Word session, Cleavant Derricks's voice may have been limited by age, his baritone may not have been as rich as it had been during World War II when he wrote "When God Dips His Love in My Heart," but the power of his spirit still moved many seasoned engineers, musicians, and onlookers to tears. This was a man who understood sacrifice, hardship, pain, and mistreatment. Yet in these words he had written each listener could also hear that he believed nothing could defeat him as long as he had Jesus by his side.

As he sang, the slight, black gentleman breathed life into every word. Embracing this opportunity to perform songs the world had cherished for so many years, Derricks used his hands to emphasize points, his voice to hit with extra power the most important words, and his eyes to share the joy he felt in his heart. Yet even amid his first opportunity to put his take on his own work, he must have been thinking back to his many years of struggle as a small-town preacher.

"When God Dips His Love in My Heart" was written when the world was at war and before the civil-rights movement had begun to open doors for Cleavant and his people. Opportunities were limited, chances at achievement were small, equal acceptance was given to only a few African-Americans of the time. So each Sunday when the Reverend Derricks rose behind his pulpit, he faced the challenge of assuring his congregation not only that God did love them but also that the suffering they faced in this world would be rewarded in the next.

Often using his own compositions to reinforce his sermons, Cleavant tried to give his people something to hang onto. In a world so ready to knock them down, Derricks knew he had to pick people up. Thus, lines such as "Sometimes tho' the way is dreary, dark and cold, and some unburdened sorrow keeps me from my goal, I go to God in prayer, and I can always find Him there" provided not only a crutch but also inspiration. Yet this song was more than just a way to help people get through a hard day; it was a vehicle for salvation, too.

In the third stanza of "When God Dips His Love in My Heart" Cleavant used Christ's trip up to Calvary's cross to remind everyone that if God could so completely give His life for us, then He isn't going to turn His back on us now. So no matter where we are or what our suffering, He is there to bring us His power, His promise, and His joy.

From 1944 to 1975 Cleavant Derricks heard his music everywhere he traveled. "When God Dips His Love" was performed by white quartets, black churches, and rock artists in almost every type of venue. The song crossed every color line and made its way into almost every music genre. Unfortunately, while the pastor could share in the joy of each new presentation, he had never shared in the financial rewards of his song's enduring popularity. Not long after he had written the song, the preacher had sold all his rights for future royalties for just enough money to purchase songbooks for his congregation. As would become the nature of his life, he short-changed himself to share God with others.

For some people this lack of sharing in what would have been hundreds of thousands of dollars in profits seemed incredibly unfair, yet as Cleavant listened to others perform "When God Dips His Love," he took no time to mourn his losses. Rather, the old preacher considered Christ's gain through the spreading of His message in song. He had composed this work to give his small congregation hope during hopeless times. He had prayed that his effort might make one life easier and one heart lighter. As he saw untold thousands brought closer to the Lord through his writing, he felt that he had reward enough. His life had never been about profits anyway; it had been about saving the lost.

In that Word studio in 1977, producer Aaron Brown couldn't help but think, *It's about time*, when he put the final touches on Derricks's first album. Yet the preacher seemed not to be concerned about the lost years of not having others hear him sing "When God Dips His Love in My Heart." As he happily told anyone who would listen, no matter who was the messenger, he was just glad the Lord had provided a way for folks to hear the message.

When the Morning Comes

He was born a slave in Maryland in 1851. Before he learned to speak, his mother died. Just after he took his first steps, his father was sold and separated from him. He was raised by other plantation servants until the conclusion of the Civil War. Then Charles Tindley was set free.

Freedom for the young boy meant plowing fields for former slave owners for fourteen hours a day, six days a week. At night, when the other men who worked alongside him sought a few hours of rest and peace, Tindley ran more than ten miles to a night school. There, in the late hours of the evening, he learned to read.

In the small church where he worshiped, it was the young Tindley who was called upon to read the congregation's tattered Bible. It was in this clapboard building filled with very poor share-croppers that the former slave began to hear the faint call to preach the gospel.

Not long after learning to read, Tindley fell in love with and married Daisy Henry. The couple moved to Philadelphia searching for job opportunities. After working a variety of odd jobs, the young man found a position as a janitor at the John Wesley Methodist Episcopal Church. Progressive, evangelical, a meeting place for Philadelphia's black community, this church was one of the largest African-American churches in the nation. As he worked and worshiped, Tindley was exposed to some of the greatest speakers and thinkers of the time. Over-come by the experience, he stepped forward to accept the call to the ministry. After studying theological courses for several more years, he began his active service.

Tindley had grown up singing in the fields. This activity, which he had once simply used to pass long, hard days, devel-oped into a passion. As a young man he sang spirituals both in the fields and in church. When he became a pastor, he quickly learned that songs could help to bring out the message of his sermons.

At first, Tindley used his rich baritone to sing established compositions and folk songs. Yet he soon found it was difficult to match songs to some of his text. Therefore, in an effort to expand the scope of his preaching, he began to write poems that matched his message. Putting music to his lyrics, he brought the major point of each of his sermons to life in song.

Tindley's songs, much like his sermons, were meant to inspire. Having lived as a slave; having faced the awesome task of trying to make a living in a world where members of his race had few opportunities for growth, expression, and advancement; being treated as a second-class citizen, shut out of jobs, schools, theaters, stores, and caf[Unknown font 1: Times New Roman Special G1]ls; and forced to accept injus-tice rather than challenge it, Tindley knew the pain of racial prejudice. He also realized that his congregation suffered this same pain every day.

"When the Morning Comes" was inspired by the questions Pastor Tindley received from his flock. These men and women wanted to know when things were going to get better, when they were going to have a chance at getting ahead. They wanted to know when the world was going to be fair. They wanted to know when the black man was going to stand beside the white man on level ground.

Tindley couldn't give his people a timetable. Nowhere in the Scripture could he find a place that spelled out the answers the former slaves and the children of former slaves wanted to know. Yet through a song he did find a way to address his people's struggles.

> *Trials dark on every hand, and we cannot understand*
> *All the ways that God would lead us to the blessed promised*
> *   land.*
> *He will guide us with his eyes and we'll follow 'til we die,*
> *And we'll understand it better by and by.*

In truth, the message Charles Tindley wrote in "When the Morning Comes" did not contain the answers his congregation wanted to hear. The church members wanted their questions answered now, not later. They wanted to have their struggles justified at this moment, not in the future. They wanted their pastor to give them something tangible they could hang onto now. Tindley wanted answers too, but all he could give his people at that moment was what he himself knew.

After Tindley first sang "When the Morning Comes" on a Sunday morning in 1904, he reminded his people that the twelve disciples who followed Christ also wanted immediate answers. They, too, wanted to level the ground and have power placed in their hands. They, too, grew tired of the trials. At first neither did they understand why they had to wait.

"When the Morning Comes" may have been meant as an aid for a single morning service at the East Calvary Methodist Church, but it quickly spread beyond those walls. Soon the song was carried to other black congregations. It must have warmed Tindley's heart to learn that in 1920 the Southern

Baptists, then a segregated union of churches, had welcomed this black preacher's words into their own hymnals. It would be a foreshadowing of things to come.

When Charles Tindley died in 1933, Thomas A. Dorsey, now considered the "Father of Gospel Music," called him the inventor of gospel music. While this fact will be debated as long as men and women come together to study Christian music, there can be no doubt that Tindley was one of the first recognized voices to put into a Christian context the struggles of African-Americans. As a matter of record, it was one of his own hymns, "We Shall Overcome," that was to become the rallying cry for the entire civil-rights movement.

Where No One Stands Alone

$\mathcal{A}$ product of the old Stamps-Baxter singing schools and an early mainstay with the Statesmen Quartet, Mosie Lister is now recognized as one of the most gifted songwriters in gospel music history. Yet there was a time in his life when just paying the bills was a mighty challenge. He and his wife and children were living hand-to-mouth, trying to save enough money from Mosie's day job to begin a publishing company and start a business serving the Lord through music. As the days of just surviving became weeks, the months became years, and the task of finally being able to make ends meet as a songwriter seemed no closer to becoming a reality, doubts couldn't help but creep into the Listers' hearts.

"I found that the job I was doing was a genuinely rewarding experience," Mosie recalled. "I was working at a piano store, meeting with customers, setting up pianos in homes and tuning them when they needed to be tuned. Yet as much as I enjoyed my work, I felt the Lord had something else in mind for me. I thought He wanted me to do more for Him."

With that thought driving him on, Mosie decided it was time to make a change. Although it made no sense to his boss or the other employees at the store, he gave up the only sure salary he had to follow the calling he felt in his heart. With no backing and no solid prospects, he began his own business.

"I started a music publishing effort," Mosie explained, "and I quit my job to do it. At this time we had the twins. Those were two mouths to feed beyond my own and my wife's, and we had bills to pay. So striking out on my own was not a smart move. But I genuinely believed that I was called by God to go into Christian songwriting and publishing. Because I believed that, I also believed He would take care of us and supply our needs."

In order to make ends meet during those lean times, Mosie traveled and performed at conventions, all-night singings, and church revivals. At times it seemed he lived on the road. Although his faith in God never wavered, doubts about his career choice must have entered his mind. As the months passed, he was working harder and harder, missing his family more and more, and seemingly getting no closer to establishing his company. A steady job tuning pianos began to look very good to him.

"I had been on a trip to South Carolina," Lister remembered four decades later, "and stopped at an all-night concert in Macon. While I was there, I talked to friends and listened to music. When the concert ended, I got into my car and began driving toward home. I wasn't really thinking about anything. I just began to sing a chorus. At first I didn't even realize that it was one I had never heard. Without knowing it, I was writing a new song. I sang it over and over, time and time again so I wouldn't forget it. The more I sang it, the more I was overcome with a spiritual feeling. After a while it seemed that I wasn't alone, that I had a choir in the car with me with an orchestra playing the music. It was an incredible experience!"

As overwhelming as his feelings had been that night, when Mosie returned home, those feelings of inspiration passed as quickly as they had come. Although he wrote down the lyrics and recorded the music to his chorus, he couldn't come up with stanzas to go with it. For a year he struggled to finish what had been so easy to begin. Finally he turned to the Bible for needed answers.

"I stumbled upon the story of David," Mosie explained, "and I identified with it strongly. I began to see David as a sinner who was feeling sorry for his sins and asking God to forgive him. I tried to take on the attitude of what I thought King David might have been feeling at that time. He was sitting alone in his palace knowing how wrong he had been; he was surrounded by the riches of the world, everything he could desire, but he was all by himself. It didn't make any difference that he was a ruler, what mattered was he was separated from God. David must have realized that nothing was worse than that. With that picture in mind, I began walking around the block, and by the time I got back I had two verses sketched out in my head."

Lister found that the two verses for which he had searched for almost a year now came as easily as the song's chorus. Quickly jotting them down, he found that the music flowed seamlessly with the lyrics. It all came together as if someone else's hand was guiding the pen.

"You know, really, this was David's testimony," Lister explained. "I really think he was something of a co-writer with me on this song. I think that is one of the keys to writing a special song—being able to put yourself so deeply into a song that you lose sight of who you are and write whatever comes into your mind. That is what happened to me with 'Where No One Stands Alone.'"

Although it might have been David's life that inspired Mosie Lister to finish a song that had come to him on a long drive, "Where No One Stands Alone" also reflects his witness at the moment of his inspiration. He was living on faith. He was swimming upstream against logic because he had answered a call. Many of those around him thought he was going to lose everything he had. Yet during moments when he didn't know how he was going to be able to pay bills, even during times when he was away from home with no one by his side, Lister realized he wasn't alone. The fact that he felt God taking each step with him gave him the faith to go on in the face of overwhelming odds. The ultimate reward of responding and sticking to that call was etched in stone not long after he had finished "Where No One Stands Alone."

"That song became a mainstay of my publishing company catalog," Lister explained. "As more and more people recorded it, it was as if God was reaffirming that He would take care of my needs and that He would always be there for me. In every trial I have had since then—losing my mother, sickness, and heartache—the words to 'Where No One Stands Alone' have come back to me and picked me up."

Mosie Lister's song of faith has served to carry a lot of people through a great many hard times. Just as when he first sang the chorus, "Where No One Stands Alone" reminds all Christians that we are never really alone. There is always Someone ready to help us carry even our heaviest loads.

Who Am I?

Rusty Goodman grew up performing with his brothers in a gospel group. He was literally singing before he could read. By the time he had hit his teens, his voice was deep, rich, and powerful. Many of those who gathered in small churches and at local fairs thought that Rusty was the standout performer in a family group filled with outstanding talent.

It was military service that called Rusty away from his Alabama home and the Goodman family. Yet being in the military didn't mean he quit singing. He continued to perform during his hitch, but instead of singing gospel music, he was lending his voice to mostly country songs. By the time he mustered out in the mid-fifties, Rusty had been caught up by the sounds of rock and roll and headed for Louisiana to work in a secular group, the Plainsmen.

The Plainsmen were a solid and entertaining quartet. They even backed up some very popular acts, including those of Jimmie Davis and Martha Carson. Yet they never generated the kind of success that elevated them to the status of the performers they backed. After a while Rusty, whose bass leads were often the most popular facet of the Plainsmen's shows, felt as though he was spinning his wheels. In five years of work, the greatest exposure he managed to receive was singing the line "way up north" on Johnny Horton's smash hit "North to Alaska."

"He was frustrated because he was not hitting the big time," explained his daughter, Tanya Goodman Sykes. "He was pursuing his dreams, but he was away from the Lord. When you had been raised like he had, that separation began to work on you. After several years with the Plainsmen, he began to feel a real pull to be reunited with family."

At first Rusty ignored the call for a homecoming. Jimmy Davis had signed him to a songwriting deal. He dedicated every spare hour to that task. He felt he could write a hit for Elvis Presley, and he knew that if Elvis recorded just one of his songs, he would have it made. Then scores of others would want him to write hits for them, too. Yet as time dragged by and the special song that had Presley's name written all over it failed to materialize, Rusty again began to look toward home.

His brothers and their families had moved to Kentucky, where Howard was pastoring a small evangelical church called the Life Temple. As the fifties gave way to the sixties, Rusty took his family there for a visit. As he listened to the sounds of the Lord's music, he realized this was not just a short stay. He had brought his family home.

"Dad now felt that he was supposed to be doing gospel music," Tanya explained, "but financially that made less sense than what he had been doing. Uncle Howard's church was just a little white cinder-block building. Vestal and Howard were just about starving themselves. They didn't have anything left over to share with us. But in spite of the fact that there were no real prospects, Dad knew he was being called and made the move to Kentucky on faith.

"At first, in spite of the fact that we had nothing, Dad was excited about doing the Lord's work. He took over the choir and created a new enthusiasm there. But after a few weeks his excitement began to wane and reality set in. Because we had no money for rent, we were living in the church's damp basement. This was not the way Dad wanted to provide for us. As time passed, I think a bit of pride began to creep in. He was in conflict. He began to ask himself, 'Have I done the right thing? Have I made a mistake?'"

Over the next few weeks Rusty grew more depressed. Every time he heard a country or a rock-and-roll song, he questioned if he had given up on his dream of being a secular songwriter too soon. He began to think that maybe he hadn't been called to full-time service for God. He wondered if living in such poverty, staying in a damp basement, and watching his children wear other people's cast-off clothes were signs that God intended him to go back to what he had been doing.

Yet deep inside, he realized the world he had left was more than just another music venue, it was a place filled with temptations. Rusty had given in to some of those temptations in the past, and if he went back into that world, he sensed he would fall again. Yet if the Lord didn't want him to go back, then he had to wonder why things were so hard right now.

"It bothered him that he had seemed to give up so easily on his dreams in secular music," Tanya recalled. "Because things were so tough, because he knew he wasn't doing a good job providing for his family, he was feeling very conflicted. Each day became a struggle. Then one morning as he was shaving in the church basement, the humbling thought hit him, 'Who am I to question the sacrifices I am making?'"

Rusty later explained that at that moment he finally realized he was following God's calling. It was also then that he realized the magnitude of God's giving His Son for every sinner.

He was completely blown away by such a concept. His own doubts about Christian service had been created because he didn't feel he was doing enough for his own children. Yet God had let His Son suffer and die for others. The more Rusty thought of this gift, the more he was humbled.

After he finished shaving he turned his revelation into song. Although first heard by only a very small congregation crowded into a tiny cinder-block church, "Who Am I?" nevertheless presented a testimony so powerful that the Spirit flooded the room. Rusty's choice of Christian service immediately seemed completely justified. Even the old basement didn't look so bad now.

"Within just a few years," Tanya recalled, "'Who Am I?' was constantly being recorded. Everyone seemed to pick it up."

For Rusty, who had simply written the song to share the news that he finally understood what the gift of salvation meant, the acclaim generated by his song was both overwhelming and humbling. Royalties offered his family a way to pay for a home, clothes, and a car. That song, along with several others he wrote later, helped give the Goodmans a ticket to sing with the giants of southern gospel music. "Who Am I?" even paved the way for Rusty to win more awards and honors than he dreamed existed. And every time one of these blessings came in, he shook his head and again wondered, "Who Am I?"

"Psalm 34:7 says that if you delight yourself in the Lord, He will give you the desires of your heart," Tanya smiled as she recited the verse. "That so fit what happened to Dad. From that morning when he realized what God had given up for him, he never concerned himself with the sacrifices he had to make. He lived for the Lord. He never wondered what could have been. The Lord gave him all he needed and more.

"Yet deep down, I still know a little part of Dad wished he could have written that big hit for Elvis. Imagine his joy when he turned on the radio and heard Elvis singing 'Who Am I?'!"

Without Him

$\mathcal{I}$t seemed only natural that Mylon LeFevre would write gospel music. His family had been one of the most respected and honored southern gospel acts of all time. His mother and father, Eva Mae and Urias LeFevre, are in the Gospel Music Association's Hall of Fame. Innovative, energetic, and driven to produce gospel music with an "edge," the LeFevres didn't just walk onto the stage, they stormed it. The power of their performances is still being talked about some four decades later.

The LeFevres were not a standard southern gospel quartet. Their music was girded by guitars, bass, drums, piano, and any other instrument they could find to play. Also, they didn't sing straight four-part harmonies. During their shows they could move from solos to duets to trios and then to quartets; then, just as quickly, they could rush into an almost choral type of country-inspired effort. There was no other group like theirs. If you needed tight structure, you wouldn't last long singing with the LeFevres. To work with them, you had to be willing to give everything you had, live spontaneously, and go wherever the Spirit moved you.

Even as a child, Mylon was the most dynamic member of this singing family. Charismatic, talented, a vocal master who also played a half dozen instruments, he had music in his blood from his days as a toddler. Wherever he performed, no matter what groups came before or followed the LeFevres, those who had gathered to hear the gospel in music left talking about the good-looking teenager. Because of his incredible talent and personality, the spotlight always seemed brighter when it shone on Mylon.

In many ways, everything might have come too easily for Mylon. He grew up gaining the approval of huge crowds, being told he was incredibly gifted, and sharing in the glory largely created by the drive and hard work of a previous generation of LeFevres. In his own mind he must have seemed immortal, a human beacon placed above those who paid to listen to him sing.

Just as being the star on stage seemed almost effortless, sharing his thoughts and ideas with others also was no problem for the young man. The first time Mylon began to compose, he seemed to effortlessly produce an exceptional work. No LeFevre had ever written anything that seemed as inspired and powerful as "Without Him."

Mylon LeFevre's strong message of depending on the Lord to guide him through each day was more a product of his imagination than actual experience. At the time he wrote the song his own faith was mostly a surface show. Religion was a product he was selling but not really using. He had little depth, spent little time in Christian growth, and sang not so much for God's glory as for his own. Nevertheless, "Without Him" was such an outstanding work that just months after it was written Elvis Presley decided to feature it on his second RCA gospel album. Because of Elvis, Mylon LeFevre, at seventeen years of age, suddenly found himself basking in more fame than almost anyone else involved in Christian music. He also quickly became very rich.

Presley's recording of "Without Him" earned tens of thousands of dollars in writer's royalties before Mylon was old enough to vote. When more than one hundred others recorded the song, he found himself floating in money. Soon he began to think of himself as a man who had all the gifts, power, and wisdom he needed. He believed God was out there, but he didn't really need Him. Those who knew Mylon well found it ironic that the earnings and acclaim showered on the young man for "Without Him" had paved the way for him to live in a world without God.

For the next fifteen years Mylon put together several bands, sang both rock and contemporary Christian music, and rubbed elbows with music's biggest stars. He partied with the likes of legendary rockers such as Alvin Lee, George Harrison, and Eric Clapton. He recorded with everyone from the Beatles to the Rolling Stones. He rode in limousines and private planes, ate at the most elegant cafés in Paris and London, and was at the heart of the jet-set lifestyle. While he may have been flying high, he was also heading for a terrifying crash. Depending on drugs to enhance his spirit, spending his money faster than he could make it, by 1970 it seemed Mylon had moved as far away from his southern gospel roots as was possible.

Three years later, now a hopeless heroin addict, LeFevre picked up a Gideon Bible while doing drugs. Alone, frustrated, whirling in a life of confusion, Mylon somehow saw in God's Word a faint light through the fog that clouded his mind. For the first time in years, a life with faith seemed to have meaning and substance, but it was not enough. Even though he once again believed God was there for him, he chose more drugs over the Savior. For seven more years he wandered along in a spiritual haze completely without Jesus.

In 1980, his career back on track and singing with a Christian musical group, "The Second Chapter of Acts," LeFevre finally sank to the bottom. With the encouragement of members of his group, he admitted to himself and his Lord that he could no longer live without a daily walk with Jesus. Falling to his knees, he begged forgiveness and pledged to live, work, and sing for God. Coming back to his roots, he accepted a call to evangelical service and spoke to thousands about his past, his sins, and his newfound hope.

For LeFevre the act of rededication almost came too late. A heart attack, caused by his years of drug abuse and his jet-set lifestyle, almost killed him before he reached his fortieth birthday. Told by doctors that two-thirds of his heart was dead and that traveling and ministering were out of the question, a weak Mylon prayed for a miracle. Now that he finally had Jesus back in his life, now that he was finally living with Him instead of without Him, he felt moved to take his message to the world. He hoped that God would somehow find a way to make this possible.

Doctors don't know how LeFevre's heart was reborn. They don't understand how a man so close to an invalid state could rebound into vital health, but most who now examine him and remember his former condition call it a miracle.

When Mylon LeFevre was just seventeen he wrote a song that would touch millions. "Without Him" is not only one of the most recorded works in gospel music history, but it has quickly found its way into countless hymnals and songbooks. It is a statement of God's power; the writer wrote the words and music to his testimony some twenty years before he understood them himself. It seems that he didn't fully grasp the power of God until he had spent half his life living without Him.

Your First Day in Heaven

For many years Stuart Hamblen's idea of fun was to party with his cowboy buddies in the bars of Los Angeles. During Hollywood's Golden Age, Hamblen was not only one of the best-known bad-guy actors in motion picture Westerns, he was also a member of an outlaw band at night. While the very stars he fought on the silver screen—men such as Roy Rogers and Gene Autry—were spending their evenings with their families, Stuart was playing poker and drinking beer. In those days the golden streets were lit by neon lights, and friends toasted days spent gambling and drinking.

The son of a Texas preacher, throughout the 1930s and much of the 1940s Hamblen seemed headed straight for an eternity in hell. He might have completely lost contact with the faith of his youth if it had not been for two people. The first was his wife, Suzy. Beautiful, confident, and self-assured, in her first fifteen years of living with one of Los Angeles's most popular party guests she never strayed from her Christian walk. Even while her husband partied, Suzy quietly presented a Christian witness in every facet of her daily life, continued active church work, and never quit praying for Stuart. Every chance she got, she gently prodded him to take another look at his life, priorities, and faith. Even after hundreds of rejections, she kept trying to gently open a door for her Lord. With faith and patience that must have rivaled those of Job, she never gave up. Even while Christian friends told her she was wasting her time, she professed that a miracle would happen.

The second person who impacted the actor/singer/radio host was a young North Carolina preacher. In 1949 Billy Graham had been booked on Hamblen's morning radio variety show. At this time Graham's tent meetings were the talk of the nation and his fiery sermons and movie star good looks were a calling card thousands could not refuse. He was a dynamo, a preacher made for a modern age. Everyone seemed to be taken by him. Even out of the pulpit and in polite conversation, the evangelist impressed Stuart. Several days after Graham's radio visit, Stuart still found himself intrigued by both the man and his mission.

Seizing upon her husband's interest in the charismatic preacher, Suzy suggested that the two of them attend one of the evening revival meetings. Stuart had to be torn by this suggestion. He had liked Graham and had been convinced that he was a sincere and dynamic individual, but what would Stuart's drinking pals say if they found out that their friend was taking in such a public sermon? How could he face their ribbing?

The one explanation Stuart needed and could claim was that he was simply going to see one of his radio guests work. Countless times he had gone to clubs to listen to the singers and see the actors who had been on his program, he had also watched many films of such actors. He could tell those who would make fun of him that this situation was no different.

It is very doubtful that Stuart expected to be caught up in the words the preacher delivered that night. It was almost beyond even his wife's belief that he might actually feel the message down deep in his soul. Yet when the choir began to sing "Just As I Am," he was one of the first to go forward. On that night, in a humble tent, he fell to his knees and gave his soul to Christ.

What had long made Stuart one of Hollywood's favorite personalities was his charm, quick wit, and easygoing manner. When he was saved, the elements that made him popular didn't change, but the way he used them did. After studying the Bible and building a foundation of understanding of how the Lord could best use him, he began to work in Graham's crusades. Frequently he gave his testimony. A seasoned songwriter with more than a dozen hits under his belt, he also naturally began to use those talents to express his Christian faith in song as well. Within days of his conversion he had written "It Is No Secret." Within five years he had established himself as one of the best country/gospel songwriters in the nation.

What Hamblen always tried to do with his music was to create lyrics that presented his feelings about life and faith. Quick with a smile and an encouraging word, he centered most of his messages on the joy of life and the wonder of salvation. Rarely did he dwell on negative thoughts, so he really was one of the original members of the "Power of Positive Thinking" club. In almost every song he wrote, this image shone through.

In 1953, while he was sitting in his home, Stuart was overcome with the happiness of knowing that his life on earth was just a small preview of the wonder that lay beyond. As he thought of Christian friends who had already died and as he considered the emotions that would flood his soul when he met them again, he began to write a story about a Christian's first day in heaven. By the time he finished those thoughts, he had composed what was to become a gospel classic that would speak to every Christian who was longing for home.

For everyone who knew the born-again Stuart, "Your First Day in Heaven" seemed the most natural song he ever wrote. This man was a dreamer who had always dreamed big dreams. As a child he had dreamed about going to Hollywood and making himself into a star. It happened. When he first arrived in town, he dreamed about being popular with all the big stars. He was. Now, when he had turned his body and soul over to Christ, he wrote about the way he dreamed heaven would be.

Stuart pictured heaven as a place of thrilling wonder. He saw smiling saints greeting him with western twangs and "How do you do!" He knew that in heaven there would be no worry and no fears, only joy, happiness, shouting, and singing. In the very best sense of the word, he saw everlasting life as a wonderful party.

Driven by its view is of a joyous heaven, the song's infectious melody and rapid-fire beat have made it one of the most performed and beloved songs of gospel music. Yet the real inspiration of "Your First Day in Heaven" is that the writer masterfully wove into the lyrics something usually reserved only for hellfire and brimstone sermons. He urged the saved not to waste their time but to study the Bible, reach out to others, and prepare for a time when all their dreams would be fulfilled. In his mind that day would begin in heaven, but his formula worked pretty well for every day spent on earth, too!

The Cathedrals
by Glen Payne and George Younce with Ace Collins

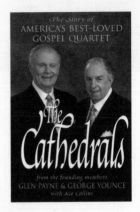

For over 30 years, the Cathedrals have shared the Gospel in song from London to New York, from the Holy Land to Nashville. Today, after more than 6,000 performances, eighty albums, and countless television appearances, they're going as strong as ever. And now the group's founders, Glen Payne and George Younce, share with you the shining peaks, the deep valleys, and enduring faith that are the story of America's most popular male gospel quartet.

Hardcover 0-310-20983-8

We want to hear from you. Please send your comments about this
book to us in care of the address below. Thank you.

ZondervanPublishingHouse
Grand Rapids, Michigan 49530
http://www.zondervan.co